THINK LIKE A BRAND, NOT A BANK

5 Practical Strategies to
Unlock Innovation, Connect
with Customers, and Grow

THINK LIKE A BRAND, NOT A BANK

Allison Netzer & Liz High

LIONCREST

PUBLISHING

Think like a Brand, Not a Bank

5 Practical Strategies to Unlock Innovation, Connect with Customers, and Grow

ISBN 978-1-5445-3124-3 *Hardcover*

978-1-5445-3123-6 *Paperback*

978-1-5445-3428-2 *Ebook*

978-1-5445-3125-0 *Audiobook*

Brand is powerful.

Forget bank-first thinking.

Brand is not soft and fluffy.

Get in touch with your feelings.

Think of Samsung with
a side of Apple.

Brand is not a marketing exercise.

Your windshield is bigger than
your rearview for a reason.

Everything builds.

Be open to odd.

Search for spaces.

Don't be customer first.

Quit fighting fintechs.

Remake meaningful moments.

Beautiful brands are born
from tension.

Modernize your roles.

Keep it simple.

Stop when you get to yes.

Make your decisions smaller.

Good things can happen in silos;
great things happen when
you break them down.

Don't ask what can we do,
ask what could we do.

Make your financial products into
brand experience.

If it doesn't work, ditch it.

Loyalty is not what it
used to be either.

Product is not brand.

Product is not a language.

Outcomes trump features,
functions, and toasters.

A mission statement is
not a mission.

Imagine if your mission
was your product.

The future of value is
shared value.

Thinking like a brand
STARTS NOW.

For my Dad, Mike Netzer,

who taught me that I don't need a

classroom to be a teacher.

—AN

For Joan High.

Look mum, I wrote a book.

Turns out you were right; I can do anything

if I just put my mind to it.

—LH

CONTENTS

INTRODUCTION   *1*

Backed by Data

Interesting, but What's in It for Me?

What You Will Learn

About Us

Why We Wrote This Book

Chapter 1

MINDSET MATTERS   *17*

Brand Is Not Soft and Fluffy

Nothing More Than Feelings

Samsung with a Side of Apple

In Brands We Trust

Brand Is Not a Marketing Exercise

Real World Example: WSFS Bank

Real World Example: Partners Federal Credit Union

Real World Example: Get Hitched

Ask Your Data to Dance

Chapter 2

PRINCIPLE ONE: SOMETIMES, DO THE COUNTERINTUITIVE THING   57

Search for Space

Does History Have a Place?

Don't Be Customer First

Real World Example: Ellevest

Quit Fighting the Fintechs

Remake Moments

Chapter 3

PRINCIPLE TWO: EMBRACE TENSION AND CREATE CONTRADICTIONS   81

Real World Example: Umpqua Bank

Modernize the Roles

Simple versus Complex

You Think You Know the Customer

Test, Learn, and Move On

Chapter 4

PRINCIPLE THREE: CUE THE REMIX   95

Real World Example: Gig Workers

Nonbanks Crash the Party

Chapter 5

PRINCIPLE FOUR: REMEMBER, PRODUCT ISN'T WHAT IT USED TO BE   105

Product Is Not a Language

FYI: Loyalty Is Not What It Used to Be Either

Product Is a Vehicle for Value

Mission As Product

Real World Example: Studio Bank

Warning! A Mission Statement Is Not a Mission

Real World Example: Chase Bank and Daylight

Making Product What It Should Be

Back to Basics: Shared Unit of Value

Real World Example: Harley Davidson

Chapter 6

PRINCIPLE FIVE: COACH AND COMPOSE _133_

Real World Example: A Moonshot in Utah

Country Music, Whiskey, and...Soccer?

Composing for a Narrow Segment

Coach to Change

Coaching Mindset

How to Coach Customers

When It Clicks

CONCLUSION _153_

ACKNOWLEDGMENTS _159_

From Allison

From Liz

INTRODUCTION

ON THE FRONT DOOR OF your neighborhood Starbucks, you see an Under New Management sign. Inside, a man in a suit and tie is greeting customers. He looks familiar. *Isn't that...?*

Jeremy, the manager of your bank?

It seems that Jeremy left the bank looking for a new challenge. He has taken over your favorite Starbucks, and implemented bold new initiatives.

"Hello!" Jeremy calls, approaching with a smile. "What can we help you with?"

"Uh...I'd like a coffee?" you say.

"Well, we can certainly help you out with that today. Is this business or personal?"

"The coffee?" You're not sure if you're on some kind of prank show. You look for cameras. "Um…personal, I guess?"

"Great! Alicia can help you with that. Station five." He points you to the last in a line of numbered barista stations.

"Hi, Alicia. Could I get a venti latte with soy milk, please?"

Alicia nods. "You betcha. We'll get you in and out in two seconds!"

You glance at the sandwiches in the display case. "Oh, and…could I add a crispy grilled cheese on sourdough?"

Alicia grimaces slightly. "Um…yeah…that's not my…" She scans the store for a moment. "Let me see if I can find you a sandwich specialist."

"What? A sandwich spec—?"

She motions to someone across the room. "Here he comes." Alicia looks relieved that she's getting some backup.

"Hi. I'm Dan," the man says. "I understand you're interested in hearing about some of our sandwich options?"

You glance around again, looking for cameras. "I'm interested in eating one of your sandwich options. That one." You point to the grilled cheese. "It's right th—"

"Follow me, please." Dan strides toward the other side of the store, which has been divided into cubicles. You look back longingly at the sandwich as you follow Dan.

He motions for you to take a seat, and types on his computer for a moment.

"Um...Dan? Sorry to interrupt. But can I...?"

Dan holds up the one sec gesture. "Just pulling up some interesting stats for you on ciabatta breads."

"No. I don't need ciabatta bread. Just that grilled cheese on sourdough. I figured...you know, with it being a cold day and all. Maybe a little comfort food..."

"I hear you," he says. "But I'd like you to keep an open mind about the possibility of moving up to a..." He cracks open a large binder and turns a few pages. He notices a Post-it Note and crumples it up. You only got a glimpse, but you could have sworn it said: "Chicken Caprese numbers lagging. Push the chicken!"

Your phone dings. It's a text from your coworker: "Can you grab me a chai tea? I'll Venmo you!"

"Do you need to reply to that?" Dan asks. "It's okay."

"No. It's just a coworker. She wants a tea."

"Coworker?" Dan says. "I'm sorry. I thought this was for personal use. Maybe I misunderstood." He motions to the manager.

"No. It's okay. Forget it," you say. But it's too late. Jeremy has arrived.

"Is there a problem?"

"She wants a business tea," Dan says, trying hard not to roll his eyes.

"I'm so sorry," Jeremy says. "I thought you said you were here for a personal coffee. If you'll just follow me."

"Wait," you say, "all I want is a latte and a grilled…" Dan is shaking his head disappointedly. As he leads you away, Jeremy is telling you that you should get overdraft protection on your Starbucks card and that, if you're thinking of investing, you should consider "shorting the scone market." And with the low broker fees, you could also…

You wake up in a cold sweat.

You breathe a sigh of relief that Starbucks, one of your favorite brands, doesn't have a banking mindset. And as you get out of bed, you wonder…

Why doesn't my bank have a brand mindset?

Although the above Starbucks dream—or maybe nightmare?—was mostly written in jest, it's not too far from how most banks operate. For banking to be more relevant in today's world, however—particularly post COVID-19—banks need to think more about creating connections and meaningful experiences for their customers. While consumer and commercial brands have been doing this successfully for decades, banks have yet to fully embrace this approach.

That's because they're still thinking like a *bank*, and not like a *brand*—and we're here to help change that.

BACKED BY DATA

Innovators and investors understand the power of brands.

Kantar, a global data and insight firm, has been valuing the world's most powerful brands (not their product or revenue; what their actual brand is worth[1]) for the last sixteen years. In their annual report, the performance of brand-led businesses during the global pandemic explicitly underlines the importance and value of thinking like a brand.

---

[1] https://www.kantar.com/campaigns/brandz-downloads/kantar-brandz-most-valuable-global-brands-2021

During the five weeks from February 14 to March 31st 2020, the MSCI World Index dropped 73 percent and the S&P 500 dropped 51 percent; a tracked portfolio of the top 150 most valuable brands dipped just 42 percent. The brand portfolio recovered its value just fifteen weeks after the COVID-19 crash in March 2020—twice as fast as the general stock market indices. And then the Strong Brands Portfolio kept on growing, gaining an additional 135 percent in value over their prepandemic peak through April 2021. Thinking like a brand is not just powerful, it drives resilience in times of uncertainty and growth in times of change.

If you compare the MSCI World Index with the S&P 500, brand focused companies did not just recover more quickly, they accelerated their growth.

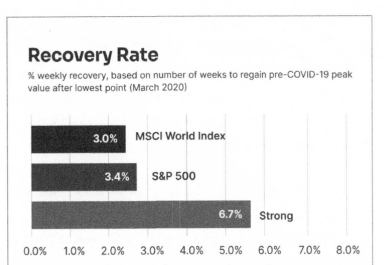

Recovery Rate

% weekly recovery, based on number of weeks to regain pre-COVID-19 peak value after lowest point (March 2020)

- MSCI World Index — 3.0%
- S&P 500 — 3.4%
- Strong — 6.7%

% RECOVERY PER WEEK

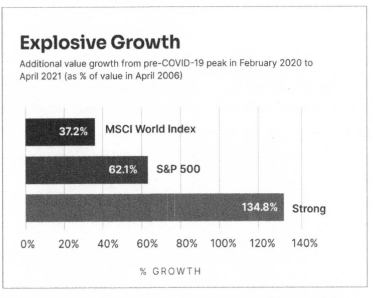

Explosive Growth

Additional value growth from pre-COVID-19 peak in February 2020 to April 2021 (as % of value in April 2006)

- MSCI World Index — 37.2%
- S&P 500 — 62.1%
- Strong — 134.8%

% GROWTH

Source: https://www.kantar.com/campaigns/brandz-downloads/kantar-brandz-most-valuable-global-brands-2021

INTERESTING,
BUT WHAT'S IN IT FOR ME?

So, point made on the importance of branding in broader industries, but you don't sell smartphones, you don't sell jeans, and you don't sell coffee. You are in financial services.

Harnessing brand power within financial services demands a new way of thinking. It's not quick, and it's not easy. But it's a shift that you can adopt—and it's worth the investment because great brands all speak the same language, and it's a language you already know.

Returns.

The Kantar study not only looked at the performance of their portfolio during the pandemic, they also looked at long-term shareholder returns. The entire portfolio (top 150 brands) has consistently outperformed the S&P 500 and the MSCI World index since tracking began.

Comparing the Kantar Brandz™

PORTFOLIO SHAREHOLDER RETURNS
2006–2021

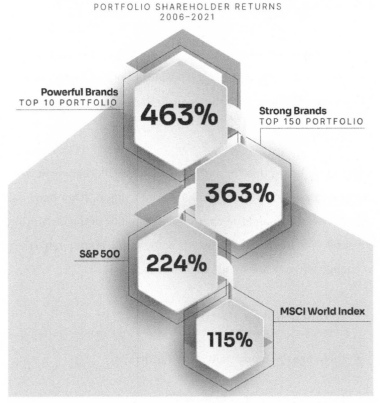

Powerful Brands
TOP 10 PORTFOLIO

463%

Strong Brands
TOP 150 PORTFOLIO

363%

S&P 500

224%

MSCI World Index

115%

Source: https://www.kantar.com/campaigns/brandz-downloads/kantar-brandz-most-valuable-global-brands-2021

The best way to think about this: If your institution had invested $1 million in an S&P tracking fund in 2006, your investment would now be worth $324 million. If you had chosen to invest in a portfolio containing the top 150 most valuable brands, you would have $463 million. And if you had—it turns out wisely—chosen to invest in just the top ten brands, your investment would have increased 463 percent, or $563 million.

Strong brands and brand thinking generate superior value for all stakeholders. Yep—inarguably, great brands get great returns.

We're talking about authentic, relevant narratives. Brands that provoke conversations and transcend business models and technology. And if your bank or credit union can do the same, you'll create real value.

You've likely heard this "brand" routine before. Perhaps you were the one to pitch it in your bank or credit union. It's a hard balance between that and the operational demands of the institution. We get it. The following represents some of the common barriers to change we've heard in our experience:

- you just don't have the budget for it

- there are too many regulatory hurdles

- it's just not how things are done

- you have legacy technology

- office politics

These are all real challenges. And we hear you!

But… here's the good news. None of these reasons block you from changing your bank's mindset. You don't need a core migration or a consultant to think like a brand. Changing the mindset won't blow out your budget. Or get regulators involved. Or be slowed down by old software. Changing the mindset from bank first to brand first is something you can do. And you can do it now.

We're going to show you how.

We want banks and credit unions to start thinking like brands so they can better connect with their customers and grow, but it starts with a mental shift (more on this in Chapter 1). Yes, you'll have to sell it internally. Yes, it will be like carrying water uphill in the beginning. But all of that work is forward moving. It's progress.

Our goal is to change the standard mentality around growth in banking and—by introducing five research-backed principles—help banks and credit unions (and those that partner with them) to think like a brand.

And yes, it starts with mindset. We've dedicated an entire chapter to mindset for a reason: none of the other principles in this book will be effective if you don't change your mindset.

WHAT YOU WILL LEARN

Over the next few chapters, we'll teach you how to think like a brand (and reap the benefits that come with it).

Some of the main points you'll learn are:

- Why mindset matters and how to shift the mindset of your institution.

- Five research-backed principles that can transform your bank or credit union.

- Real-life examples of successful, excuse-proof applications of each principle.

- How to introduce and implement change to better meet future needs.

All of the principles you'll learn about build on one another, so we recommend reading this book from start to finish and not skipping ahead. Our principles will take you from viewing people as bank customers with financial needs, to viewing (and treating) them as customers with multiple affinities and motivations. This, in turn, will lead to innovation and growth.

We know this, because we've seen it countless times.

ABOUT US

Meet Allison

I started my career at Dell, working across a range of cross-industry sales and marketing roles in the US, India, and Japan. Over the past two decades, I have had the privilege of working with brands like the Dallas Cowboys, Cisco, Southwest Airlines, and Aetna. In 2015, I made the shift to financial services and joined Kony, Inc., bringing a brand-first perspective to vendors and customers alike.

In 2015, I made the shift to financial services and joined Kony, Inc., co-creating the leading digital banking SaaS brand in the US before acquisition by Temenos. At Nymbus, we're on a mission to create value and growth in financial services and beyond through new ways of thinking, many of which you'll find in this book.

One of my favorite parts of working in financial services is the opportunity to do the counterintuitive thing, and this has been a guiding principle in my approach to the brands I help create.

Meet Liz

In the course of my marketing career, I have worked with virtually every industry, using data-driven insight to help shape corporate strategy. I love research, and always approach problem solving from a data-driven point of view. I have founded and co-founded successful consulting firms, and over the years my clients have included everyone from tech giants Microsoft and Amazon, to entertainment heavyweight HBO.

Luckily, thinking like a brand is my day job. As a transplant from the UK, my job gives me the privilege of experiencing the diverse people, landscapes, and cultures that my adopted nation has to offer. I have three rules for getting to know a new client's context: visit a local brewery and talk to the regulars, watch a local sports team play, and most importantly, find the best local diner in town and make friends with the waitstaff. All the best brands I've created started with a great conversation.

WHY WE WROTE THIS BOOK

We have spent years showing banks, credit unions, and fintechs how to leverage the power of a brand mindset to drive growth. And we've done this mostly through one-to-one conversations. We've helped a lot of folks, but at this rate, we'll be 150 years old by the time we've reached each banker individually.

So, it is time to scale out our message to reach more people. We'd also like to start a wider conversation—perhaps even a healthy debate —in the financial sector about how to best meet the challenges of our changing industry.

Allison views marketing as mostly about momentum and emotion, whereas Liz views it more from a data perspective. As such, working together, we tend to approach things from opposite ends of the spectrum—which puts us at an advantage. One reason we've been able to create award-winning solutions and a lot of momentum for financial brands is because when we meet in the middle—something that works from an emotional and a data-driven point of view—it's proven to be wildly successful.

And in the pages that follow, you're going to find out why.

Although we will touch on marketing, this is not a marketing book. You do not need to be a marketer to benefit from this book.

Not everyone needs to be a marketer, but everyone does need to think like a brand—and that starts with changing your mindset, which we'll dive into in the next chapter.

Chapter 1

MINDSET MATTERS

"Those who cannot change their minds
cannot change anything."

—George Bernard Shaw

THIS MAY COME AS A GREAT SHOCK TO YOU, but bankers tend to think about banking.

Loans, savings accounts, checking accounts, risk.

In short...

Selling products the bank wants to sell. (Remember Jeremy and Dan from the Starbucks story?)

Banks tend to have a product mindset, but this doesn't match customer behavior.

Do you know anyone who switches back and forth between iPhones and Samsung Galaxy with each upgrade to get the best, newest technology? Probably not.

We're not saying that banks don't think about customers. They absolutely do! They feel that because their products are great and their rates are competitive, they're going to make their customers very happy. They firmly believe that being customer centric is about delivering the best products and returns.

And yes, that's one part of the banking equation, but not all.

The traditional mindset is: "If you build it, they will come." But, we know that the old axiom isn't necessarily true today. People don't consume financial services in the way that they used to.

The paradigm has shifted.

Some banks saw the paradigm changing, and responded by taking everything in their brick-and-mortar branches and putting it online. The old customer experiences were now on laptops and mobile phones, and instead of advertising no-fee checking on huge printed banners outside their branches, banks could now say it in banner ads.

The shift didn't end there either. Websites changed from flashing interest rates to showcasing smiling people, but the mindset was still bank-first...loans, checking accounts, savings accounts, risk.

Because banks think like banks. Here's how to change that.

BRAND IS
NOT SOFT AND FLUFFY

Let's try an experiment.

Think about your brand. What is your brand like? How would you describe it?

Now, just curious...did you think of your logo? Or your tagline? Did you picture your website?

Traditionally, *brand* has been associated with visual imagery, and that perception still exists today.

Let's try another exercise: name a brand that's about more than its logo. A brand that people equate with an attitude. Or an emotion. Or a way of life.

Got one?

Okay. Was it Wells Fargo? (Hey. We heard that. Someone laughed.) Or was it something like Apple, Jeep, Patagonia, Nike, or Coca-Cola?

Powerful brands go beyond pictures. They recognize that brand is not soft and fluffy; it's a value driver.

We previously mentioned how Kantar, a global data and insight firm, releases an annual report on the valuation of the world's biggest brands (not their product or revenue; what their actual brand is worth). And in the case of Amazon, it's worth over $683 billion.

The Visa and Mastercard brands are worth over $191 billion and $112 billion, respectively.

Visa and Mastercard have proven that financial services companies can build value with a recognizable, defined brand. But they aren't banks. No bank has ever cracked the top fifty in Kantar's report. The highest bank brand value is Industrial and Commercial Bank of China (ICBC) at $37 billion, and it is ranked fifty-first—nineteen spots below Marlboro cigarettes.

So why can't banks add value by focusing on brand?

Well, they can!

In an unofficial straw poll of our coworkers, we asked which companies came to mind when it came to brand-first thinking. Naturally, we got a wide range of responses that included brands from vastly different categories: Patagonia, Square, BMW, and Maker's Mark. Two of the responses—Ritz-Carlton and Zappos—were hardly surprising, considering that they've become almost legendary for their devotion to their customers.

So what is the mission of Zappos? As they put it, "our purpose is simple: to live and deliver WOW.…providing the very best customer service, customer experience, and company culture."[2]

And Ritz-Carlton? Their mission is also clear. "The Ritz-Carlton is a place where the genuine care and comfort of our guests is our highest mission."[3]

There is no "save the planet" or "work toward a more just society" in their mission statements. The mission is the customer. The customer is the mission.

Zappos and Ritz-Carlton both empower their employees to do whatever it takes to meet the needs of their customers. At Zappos, even a customer service rep in a call center has the power to fix problems for the shopper. They have the authority to process refunds, send replacement products as overnight shipments, or even help the customer find a product on competitors' websites.

---

[2] https://www.zappos.com/about/

[3] https://www.ritzcarlton.com/en/about/gold-standards

Similarly, the staff at each Ritz-Carlton hotel has been given carte blanche to make their guests happy. The company has empowered (and encouraged) their employees to spend up to $2,000 per guest to ensure that each customer has a superior experience during their stay.[4]

When customers are the mission, there is a high level of advocacy on behalf of the organization. After all, word of mouth advertising runs wild after a legendary customer service experience. Advocacy attracts new customers. But, advocacy combined with a deeply personal mission is even more powerful.

NOTHING MORE THAN FEELINGS

Brand is what customers think and feel when they hear a company's name. It is the cumulative effect of every message, exposure, and experience that a person has with them.

When we say Jeep, what comes to mind?

How about Patagonia? Nike? Coca-Cola?

---

[4] https://ritzcarltonleadershipcenter.com/2019/03/19/the-power-of-empowerment/

Chances are these brands make you think and feel about experiences, goals reached, or people that you have spent time with.

In order for a brand to have strong value, the organization must connect with customers on an emotional level. And this is more than just a theory, or something that only applies to shampoo or cereal, it's backed by research.

A cross-industry study published by *Harvard Business Review* showed customers that felt a true emotional connection with the brands they did business with were 52 percent more valuable (i.e., spent more, shopped more, invested, borrowed, and saved more) than those that had a purely functional brand relationship. When customers are connected emotionally to a financial brand, their lifetime value is 35 percent higher.

Yes, we said *emotionally connected* to financial services.

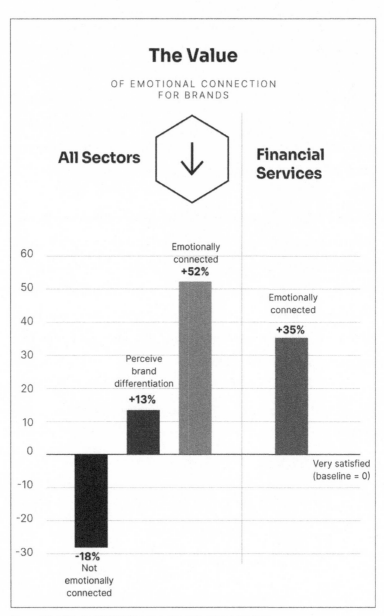

The Value

OF EMOTIONAL CONNECTION
FOR BRANDS

All Sectors

Financial Services

Emotionally connected **+52%**

Emotionally connected **+35%**

Perceive brand differentiation **+13%**

Very satisfied (baseline = 0)

-18% Not emotionally connected

Source: https://hbr.org/2015/11/the-new-science-of-customer-emotions

THINK LIKE A BRAND, NOT A BANK

SAMSUNG WITH A SIDE OF APPLE

So, how do you create emotional connection as a bank brand? Let's look at iPhone and Samsung as an example.

Both brands offer similar products and services, but the reason Apple is number two in Kantar's most valuable brands, with $6.1 billion compared to Samsung, who ranked forty-second at $0.4 billion, is the degree of emotional connection with the brand (not the smartphone). This is a classic example of a brand-first mindset.

Once customers find an experience that matches their needs and resonates emotionally, they're more likely to have a high level of trust in the brand offering that experience, which then opens them up to investing further in that relationship. In other words, they have found their tribe.

And Apple has done that successfully. They've created a massive tribe.

If people choose a tribe when it comes to smartphones, then they choose a bank based on the best offer, right?

Maybe they used to, but that has changed. Just take a look at digital upstarts like Current.

Current is a digital banking solution specifically designed for parents with teens or tweens. It allows parents to dole out weekly or monthly allowances digitally, and then track how they're spent. The parent can track their teens' purchases, block certain merchants (oh, *hell no*, you're not shopping at a vape store), and even set up chores that they can be rewarded for completing. And here's the kicker…

It pays no interest, and it has an annual fee.

But people are signing up and paying for the service, because they have connected emotionally with the brand. It's a brand that stands for good parenting, and there are plenty of people out there who can relate to that. It's not a transactional decision. It's an emotional decision based on "We like what you folks are doing there at Current" and "You really get me. You know what makes life easier for a parent."

Finding your tribe is not based on efficiency. It's not transactional. It's emotional.

And perhaps more importantly, it is the emotional connection that builds trust—but even the best of us still need to work on our trust issues.

IN BRANDS WE TRUST

The 2021 Edelman Trust Barometer is an annual study that gauges the level of trust that consumers have in key industry sectors (that surveys more than 33,000 interview respondents in twenty-eight countries). The study categorizes responses into three cohorts: distrust (1-49 percent of population say they trust the sector), neutral (50-59 percent trust), and trust (60-100 percent express trust for the sector).

As depicted in the graph, things were looking pretty good for financial services globally right up to the pandemic. Although still very much in the neutral zone, financial services trust was steadily climbing and following a similar trajectory to businesses overall.

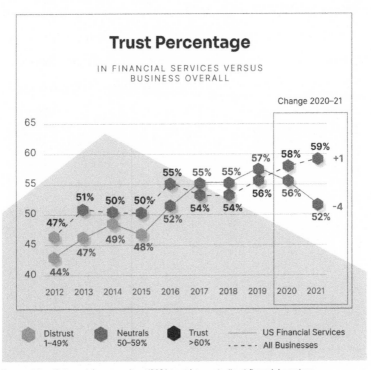

Source: https://www.edelman.com/trust/2021-trust-barometer/trust-financial-services

Enter 2020. Enter the pandemic.

While trust in other industries continued to climb during the peak of COVID-19, financial services scores dropped to just two percentage points above a distrust classification, with a full seven points separating the industry from business as a whole by the end of 2021.

Not a great story, but something really interesting happened for a few short months in 2020.

Between January 2020 and May the same year, trust in US financial services businesses rose seven points, catapulting them into the trust zone for the first time since the study began. Sixty-one percent of US consumers said they trusted the financial services sector.

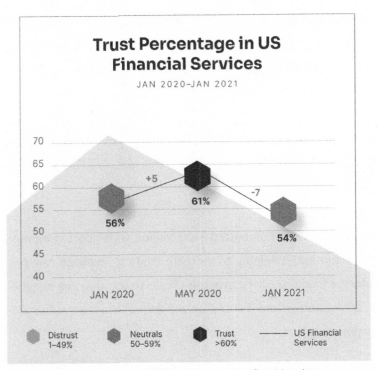

Trust Percentage in US Financial Services

JAN 2020–JAN 2021

+5

61%

-7

56%

54%

JAN 2020   MAY 2020   JAN 2021

Distrust 1–49%   Neutrals 50–59%   Trust >60%   ——— US Financial Services

Source: https://www.edelman.com/trust/2021-trust-barometer/trust-financial-services

This upward trend in trust correlates with banks, community banks in particular, and credit unions stepping in with the Paycheck Protection Program (PPP), which provided loans, mortgage forgiveness initiatives, and community support to keep the economy going and their customers afloat.

By May 2020, over $800 billion had been distributed in PPP loans. Almost every institution had payment forgiveness in place on all their major lending products, and the press was full of stories about banks offering unprecedented local and national support.

For example, Ally donated $3 million to help those impacted by COVID-19, including food distribution, health care, emergency housing, and childcare in their hometown locations of Detroit and Charlotte.

Bank of California partnered with the not-for-profit Food Finders to provide over 300,000 meals to vulnerable groups across Southern California.

Bank of America committed $100 million to support communities nationwide, helping to increase medical response capacity, address food insecurity, increase access to learning as a result of school closures, and focused on supporting the most vulnerable populations first.

This was new bank thinking. This was new bank behavior. This was emotional, empathetic, and meaningful. This was how brands would respond, not banks. People took note. People liked it.

But unfortunately, it didn't last. By the end of 2021, the trust score was down seven points.

Why? Emotional gestures have a short shelf life.

A brand mindset is not about initiatives; it's a systemic mindset that shapes your response to everything you do, not just the big moments.

Take Patagonia, for example. For those with a passion for the out-doors, or who want to look good while wandering around Central Park, this brand is an obsession. The power of the brand is not the products it sells, although they are exceptional; it is the way that the company was built, and the mindset it operates with every day.

Let's start with the fact that Patagonia has a director of philosophy. Vincent Stanley has been guiding the mindset of the company and driving it towards its $1 billion valuation for almost ten years.

Pause for a second. Imagine just how different your next board meeting might be if it was chaired by someone with that job title. (Don't worry, we will come back to this later in Chapter 3.)

Patagonia's mission is also refreshingly simple: "We are in business to save our home planet."

And it is not just words. They consistently put their money where their mouth is, donating 1 percent of their sales every year to support grassroots environmental organizations. In 2021, they went a step further. After breaking all company records with $10 million in sales during their Black Friday event, they gave every single penny to environmental groups around the world.

They charge a premium for their products because they can. They have invested heavily in research and development to invent and perfect consistently high quality, high performing, and sustainably produced sport equipment. Ninety-four percent of their line is produced using recycled materials, and they are actively striving to make it 100 percent. Over 64,000 workers are supported by their participation in the Fair Trade program. One hundred percent of their electricity needs in the US are met with renewable energy.

They also openly address any issues that put their philosophy and belief system at risk. For example, after they were criticized for using goose down collected from live animals, they now source only down that is certified to the Advanced Global Down Standard. They don't just talk, they act, so their customers trust them explicitly because they approach every decision and every action with intention.

Now, think about the multitude of vendors you work with on a daily basis. Thinking like a brand actually helps you find great partners and increases your efficiency at the same time.

When you show the world a mission-based brand, you will automatically attract partners who are aligned with your values. Instead of spending countless hours vetting vendors to determine whether they are a good match for your company's values, your mission will bring the right kind of partner to you. Think of all those hours you spend evaluating and performing due diligence on every potential vendor—even down to your coffee supplier.

Imagine how thinking (and acting) like a brand could quickly narrow the field. If you're committed to equal pay, for example, you could rule out a majority of vendors right off the bat. The companies that just don't get your mission can be crossed off the list immediately, saving you that time-consuming investigatory work.

And as you connect with other companies who share your mission, you will form an ecosystem of organizations with values that are well aligned with your customers. Your vendors will understand the brand, and knowing that you share their values, they'll give you their best work.

If you take a look at the most successful consumer brands outside of the financial sector, you'll see that their partners—the marketing agency, the tech vendors, and even down to the window designers in retail—usually reflect their key values.

BRAND IS NOT A MARKETING EXERCISE

When banks and credit unions consider their brand, it is often in the context of a marketing campaign.

It's easier to think about brand as part of a campaign, because campaigns have a beginning and an end. They have a budget, timeframe, and performance metrics. (Remember the move from branch to online banking?)

There are two fundamental problems with this strategy.

Relegating brand only to marketing places your institution's identity (and ability to create value) in the hands of a single department. Brand, however, belongs to every single person in the organization.

Brand can be broken up into two pieces: brand identity and brand personality. Brand identity is what most people think about when they think about brand—the name, the logo, the colors, the images, and the voice and tone in their email marketing and social media posts.

Brand personality, however, goes deeper than that. Brand personality encompasses everything customers can't see—your Why, your mission, and your vision. It's who you are and how you operate, not just how you look.

Successful brands have both identity and personality. They work together to create emotional connections with their customers. Brand personality is the emotional and human association with a brand, whereas brand identity is the image created to evoke a reaction from audiences.

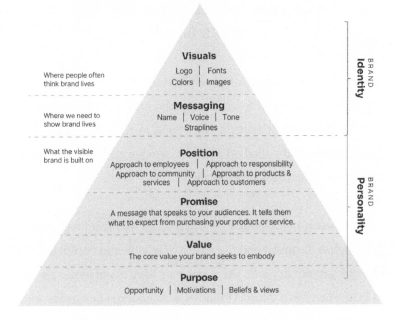

Visuals
Logo | Fonts
Colors | Images

Where people often
think brand lives

BRAND
Identity

Messaging
Name | Voice | Tone
Straplines

Where we need to
show brand lives

What the visible
brand is built on

Position
Approach to employees | Approach to responsibility
Approach to community | Approach to products &
services | Approach to customers

Promise
A message that speaks to your audiences. It tells them
what to expect from purchasing your product or service.

BRAND
Personality

Value
The core value your brand seeks to embody

Purpose
Opportunity | Motivations | Beliefs & views

This is why mindset matters. Your brand is the strategy of the organization, reflected in every decision you make, regardless of department. It influences your valuation, the way your employees interact with customers, and how you tell your story in the market.

Brand thinking is not a marketing exercise. It doesn't have a timeframe. It's something that every person in your organization has to adopt. They have to live it and breathe it.

REAL WORLD EXAMPLE:
WSFS BANK

Diving into how to move from bank first to brand first, we spoke at length with our friend Justin Dunn, who is Senior Vice President and Chief Marketing Officer at WSFS Bank. Justin is a seasoned bank marketer and had pulled off a Moses-sized miracle in rebranding a very traditional East Coast bank.

One of Justin's challenges at WSFS Bank was the bank name—Wilmington Savings Fund Society. It was long and confusing. No one quite understood it. The name may have made perfect sense in 1832 when the bank was founded, but modern consumers were not connecting with it. So, Justin's team launched a rebrand.

WSFS set out to give the public a new take on the name, and a new perception of the bank as a whole. In a coordinated campaign of TV spots, WSFS was pronounced "WissFiss"—something infinitely more accessible than "Wilmington Savings Fund Society." The tagline, We Stand For Service, gave customers all they needed to know about what the letters stood for. In addition to a catchy new nickname, the campaign gave the audience a narrative. The ads didn't focus on mortgage rates. They didn't focus on no-fee checking accounts. They told a *story*. "Things are getting bigger. National. International. Global," the voice-over states, but "At WissFiss, we still believe in being local...and the service that comes with it. Knowing the community because we grew up here."

As Justin says, "When you bring people along for the journey through the story, that's when people start viewing you more as a lifestyle brand than a bank."

The rebranding campaign took a liability—a confusing name that no one understood—and turned it into an asset. When Justin's team surveyed the community, they found that brand awareness had skyrocketed. At that point, many financial institutions would end the campaign, file the project as mission accomplished, and move on to the next thing.

Justin, however, understood the difference between bank-first mindset and brand-first mindset. He encouraged leadership at WSFS to continue funding the campaign even after it had achieved its objectives. He worked hard to communicate and educate internally that if you don't keep feeding the brand, it can fade and awareness will drop.

It wasn't just a marketing campaign. It was brand.

Getting the message of brand identity to the community is an ongoing mission. Instead of saying "mission accomplished," a brand-minded company says, "This is who we are *now*." It wants to continue to build on the awareness they've created and make the brand pervasive in people's lives—and that's what Justin pushed for.

Internally, WSFS continued to sell the brand-first mindset to employees as well. Justin recognized that a brand's most important assets walk out the door (or log off) every night. Brand is not a logo. Brand is not a color. Brand is your people. You have to have your people on board to reflect your brand. Justin understood that brand mindset is not a marketing exercise, it's about the entire institution.

"The marketing department is the largest department in the bank because everyone is part of the marketing department," Justin shared with us. "Everyone is a reflection of your brand." If you have successfully sold this message to your people, you will find that they are not just proud of their job, they are proud of their bank. The goal is to have your crew thinking, "I'm not proud to be a teller, I'm proud to be a teller at XYZ bank." It's a small distinction, but it makes an enormous difference.

Through a coordinated rebranding campaign, dedication to an ongoing public message, and a brand-first mindset in house, WSFS went from thinking like a bank to thinking like a brand.

REAL WORLD EXAMPLE:
PARTNERS FEDERAL CREDIT UNION

We also sat down with John Janclaes, who was the President & CEO of Partners Federal Credit Union for almost seventeen years.

Partners FCU serves employees of the Walt Disney Corporation and its subsidiaries and, as you can imagine, has a sizable membership, with more than 180,000 members.

John was with Partners during the 2000s and 2010s, when the credit union was undergoing a massive digital transformation. So how did they create a brand-first mindset with so much upheaval going on? For John, the key was sticking to one important ground rule.

A mindset shift, according to John, is not about how you see the world, it's understanding how others see it.

John figured that if the mindset shifted during their digital transformation, then the brand (i.e., everything) would shift with it, because brand is more than just marketing. Brand is the collective attitude and essence of the organization.

You have to try to see the world the way your customers see it. "We can know a lot by being customers ourselves, experiencing the real world and staying curious," John said.

When you think like a brand and shift to seeing your world the way your customers see theirs, you can create a real connection. But how do you know you have that connection? John has a four-point test. The brand connection is there when you can honestly say:

- I identify with it.

- I'm integrated with it.

- I care about it.

- It matters to me.

At this point, we can almost hear a protest from one or two of our readers. "Easy for you to say. You talk to all these people who make revolutionizing an institution look easy. There are so many reasons it will be harder for me. For starters, I just don't have the board support."

It's not exactly true that John had an easier time instilling a brand mindset at Partners. "It's hard to see things as they really are. It takes energy to get that perspective, and so most people assume technology alone can solve their problem. You have to fight for clarity. You have to fight for members. You have to fight for your brand."

All of the reasons that it can't be done—the deep down feelings that it just couldn't work at your institution—are called limiting beliefs. In our experience, people tend to find more reasons not to do something than to do it, and that's a big reason why we decided to write this book. We believe there is no such thing as barriers to growth, only opportunities not taken.

REAL WORLD EXAMPLE: GET HITCHED

The president of the bank enters the conference room, and everyone instinctively sits up straight. He looks the part of a bank president—with a blue pinstripe suit, a black leather portfolio, and the expected amount of gray hair that comes with forty-three years of service. He carries himself with all the seriousness and gravitas of a man who is trusted with the financial security of an entire town.

He takes his place at the head of the table, opens his portfolio, and…

Bridal magazines spill out.

The president doesn't blush, or hastily cram them back into his folder. He simply shrugs.

"This is an exciting opportunity," he says.

Walter "Chip" Hasselbring III is the President and CEO of Iroquois Federal in Watseka, Illinois. He's a banker in the classic sense of the term, and he knows how to run a bank. In his decades with Iroquois Federal, he has seen his community bank grow. Not only do they serve Watseka, but also seven other communities.

But how much can a community bank grow? Finding new customers in established markets is hard, especially when you're already doing business with many of them.

Iroquois Federal has long been committed to providing the efficiency and convenience of modern technology supported by people-backed relationships. Now Chip and Iroquois COO Linda Hamilton have found a way to branch out without additional brick and mortar. They've decided to focus on a very specific segment of customers…newlyweds. Helping people starting a new relationship build a stronger and successful lasting relationship.

In an effort to expand their hometown community bank experience, Iroquois has launched a new digital brand in a space that has plenty of room for growth. With annual revenue of $57 billion, the wedding business is a big market, and this digital brand enables Iroquois Federal to expand from a footprint of thousands, to a prospect pool of over two million newlyweds per year.

The new digital venture is called Hitched, and it aims to serve the specific, unique financial needs of new couples—from adjusting to the new experience of a joint bank account, to setting financial goals.

But in order to make this thing work, Chip and Linda are immersing themselves in everything bridal, everything wedding, and everything newlywed. They are reading, researching, and talking to people who are newly engaged or married in order to get inside the heads of their customers and understand what they are experiencing. Preparing to launch Hitched has required a different mindset—they are thinking differently, which has been energizing for Chip and Linda.

Iroquois Federal already knew how to grow a bank by offering a wide range of products and services to a broad base of customers across all age groups, but now they're thinking like a brand, and are poised to become the bank for a distinct group of customers who are ready to "Get Hitched."

ASK YOUR DATA TO DANCE

Banks know a lot about you. They know where you shop. They know when you shop, and how much you spend. They know the brands you're connected with. They know when your birthday is.

Banks have an abundance of super-rich data.

In our experience, however, financial institutions don't take a brand-first lens to their data. Instead, they have a bank or product focus, emphasizing things like credit score, bank balance, and products per household.

If you look at how supermarkets are using data, for example, you'll see that they take a different approach—and they know their customers far more intimately than the average bank or credit union.

The largest grocery chains, such as Tesco in the UK, or Kroger in the US, gather mountains of consumer data with their loyalty card programs. When their customers sign up for a loyalty card (and all the great deals that come with it), they give permission to the company to gather and use their data. This means, in the case of Tesco, that they are able to assemble data on the shopping habits of close to 20 million households, and for context, there are only 27.8 million households in the whole country. So they have deep behavioral data on 72 percent of the UK's population.

Not only can Tesco use the data to more effectively target offers and deals, but they can also learn the times of highest consumer traffic in order to staff their stores more strategically.

Banks have exactly the same data, but not just for Tesco or Kroger. They have it for every single supermarket. And every retail store. And online commerce. Banks have the power to know their customers better than anyone. And to really understand their customers better. It's strange that the store selling you lettuce knows far more about you than the company that's going to help you buy a home—and that's why mindset matters.

Utilizing the available data, banks could be more creative with their offerings to customers. If a bank notices spending patterns indicating that a couple has suddenly started shopping at BuyBuy Baby, it could be a clue that something big has just happened in their lives. But could it be a new niece or nephew? Was it for a friend's baby shower? If the bank can also find data showing that the couple's income lowered, they can guess that one person might have given up work for a period of time. They can validate the couple's age group and determine that...these two customers probably had a baby.

Many banks reach out to customers to address probable life events, but based solely on demographics. As soon as a customer turns eighteen, they're tossed in the "student" bucket and start receiving information on student loans. Customers from age twenty-two to thirty-two get thrown into the "probably getting married and want to buy their first home" bucket. Most organizations aren't using any context with the demographic data, so they can be wildly off target in their marketing.

Let's look at two celebrities with the same demographics as an example. Prince Charles and Ozzy Osbourne look exactly the same on paper. They were both born in 1948 in England. They both have two children and have been married twice. And they're both wealthy, having found success in their various business dealings.

But they are anything but the same.

The Risk

OF RELYING ON DEMOGRAPHICS

Born in 1948
Grew up in England
Married Twice

2 Children
Successful in business
Wealthy

Prospect 1
PRINCE CHARLES

Prospect 2
OZZY OSBOURNE

Imagine what your bank would offer Prince Charles and Ozzy Osbourne if you relied only on data segmentation or personalization software…

When you make better use of the available data, you can start to see the customer through a much broader lens…you can see a whole person, not just their demographics or transactions with your bank.

If you know your customers better, you can reach out to help them with the life events they're facing. And when you reach out to help, you can form stronger bonds. And stronger bonds mean a stronger brand. And a stronger brand means your institution is worth more.

If you still need convincing, remember that your windshield is bigger than your rearview for a reason.

There is only so much that can be achieved by looking at what has already happened. Real opportunity comes from looking ahead, and to do that effectively, you need to dance with your data. That means advancing your analytics, and developing a data-led approach.

It is worth it, but don't just take our word for it.

A 2020 study from the Melbourne Business School showed that investing in evolving analytics practices delivers both superior growth and profitability. Yes, we are back to brand thinking delivering returns again.

The study analyzed over 300 companies from forty countries and thirty-three industries with a median revenue of $300 million, and categorized them into four stages along the following analytics maturity curve:

The Analytics Maturity Curve

IN THE US BANKING INDUSTRY

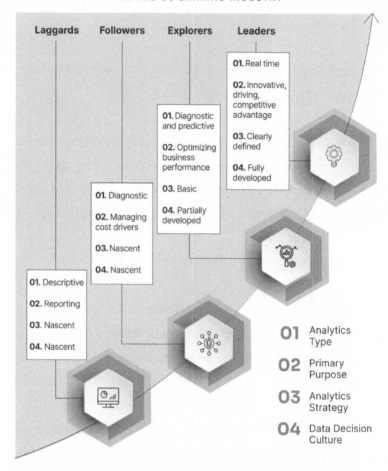

Laggards	Followers	Explorers	Leaders
01. Descriptive	**01.** Diagnostic	**01.** Diagnostic and predictive	**01.** Real time
02. Reporting	**02.** Managing cost drivers	**02.** Optimizing business performance	**02.** Innovative, driving, competitive advantage
03. Nascent	**03.** Nascent	**03.** Basic	**03.** Clearly defined
04. Nascent	**04.** Nascent	**04.** Partially developed	**04.** Fully developed

01 Analytics Type

02 Primary Purpose

03 Analytics Strategy

04 Data Decision Culture

Source: https://www.kearney.com/analytics/article/?/a/the-impact-of-analytics-on-the-triple-bottom-line

Looking at the maturity model and your current approach to customer analytics, where would you be? Laggard, follower, or seeing the benefits of advanced analytics today?

If you picked the two lower stages, don't worry; you are in good company. In a 2020 report by the Financial Brand, they found that most financial institutions did not rank themselves very highly on data maturity.

While most organizations recognized that they had a lot of data, just over a quarter felt that they were strong on data accessibility, but only 18 percent felt that they were strong at using insight.

The Levels Of Data Maturity

IN THE US BANKING INDUSTRY

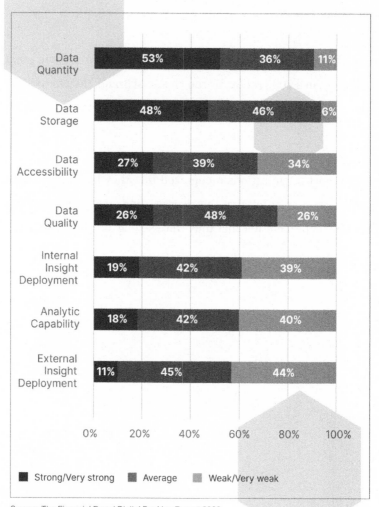

	Strong/Very strong	Average	Weak/Very weak
Data Quantity	53%	36%	11%
Data Storage	48%	46%	6%
Data Accessibility	27%	39%	34%
Data Quality	26%	48%	26%
Internal Insight Deployment	19%	42%	39%
Analytic Capability	18%	42%	40%
External Insight Deployment	11%	45%	44%

■ Strong/Very strong   ■ Average   ■ Weak/Very weak

Source: The Financial Brand Digital Banking Report 2020

THINK LIKE A BRAND, NOT A BANK

So it is an acknowledged industry challenge, but cracking big data delivers returns. The Melbourne Business School's study showed that analytics laggards could increase their overall profit by an average of 81 percent if they were to increase their maturity to the level of leaders. The potential overall profit increase for followers is 55 percent, while the profit potential for explorers is 25 percent.

It is time to think more deeply about your data. It's time to look forward and beyond traditional demographics and psychographics. Yes, you guessed it: it's time to think (and analyze) more like a brand.

KEY TAKEAWAYS

Mindset Matters

1. **Brand is powerful:** Brand-first businesses deliver superior returns. Fact.

2. **Forget bank-first thinking:** The days of "If you build it, they will come" are over. They won't.

3. **Brand is not soft and fluffy:** Brands can add billions to your balance sheet. Just ask Mastercard and Visa.

4. **Get in touch with your feelings:** connecting emotionally with your bank customers drives revenue.

5. **Think of Samsung with a side of Apple:** don't build a new product, form a tribe.

6. **Brand is not a marketing exercise:** Your brand is your Why. Your mission. It's who you are.

7. **Your windshield is bigger than your rearview for a reason:** open your aperture and go beyond financial metrics to deliver meaningful customer experiences.

The rest of the book will dive into the principles we've found successful in helping financial institutions think more like a brand. We've dedicated a chapter to each principle.

The next five chapters will teach you how to:

1. Sometimes, do the counterintuitive thing.

2. Embrace tension and create contradictions.

3. Cue the remix.

4. Remember, product isn't what it used to be.

5. Coach and compose.

Before we dive into what it means to do the counterintuitive thing, a quick reminder that the principles in this book build on one another. If you haven't absorbed Chapter 1, it will be hard to do the other steps.

In fact, if you do counterintuitive things without knowing why you're doing them, you will probably not help your brand grow. Actions that are counterintuitive without being brand focused will not only seem out of place, they'll appear downright nuts—like playing golf in a thunderstorm.

But when you've embraced thinking like a brand, doing the counterintuitive thing will feel more natural, which we'll cover in the next chapter.

54 THINK LIKE A BRAND, NOT A BANK

Mindset matters.

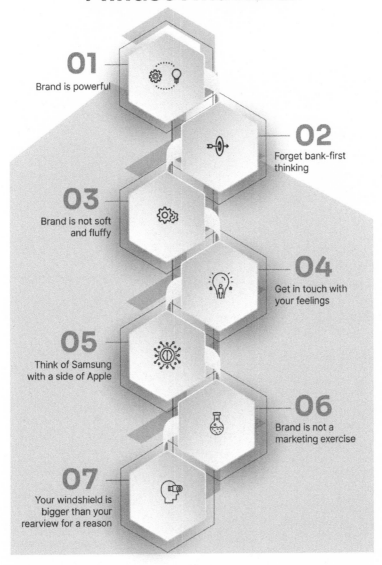

01 Brand is powerful

02 Forget bank-first thinking

03 Brand is not soft and fluffy

04 Get in touch with your feelings

05 Think of Samsung with a side of Apple

06 Brand is not a marketing exercise

07 Your windshield is bigger than your rearview for a reason

Chapter 2

PRINCIPLE ONE: SOMETIMES, DO THE COUNTERINTUITIVE THING

"Sometimes things don't make sense until the end of the story."

—Bill & Ted Face the Music

LET'S SAY YOU WORK AT the headquarters of a credit union—a sizable credit union, in fact, with fourteen locations and $2.41 billion in assets. And your career is going well. Recently, the president of the credit union hinted that he might pull you in to help with a new project he's about to roll out.

You're dying to know what this opportunity is, so when he calls you later in the week, you answer immediately, even though you're still in the parking garage.

"Hey," he says, "Ready to _____ that project I mentioned?"

Damn it. The call is cutting in and out. You hustle toward the garage exit. "Yes, of course!" you say.

"That's great!" he says, "Because we're _____ a new mobile experience. It's going to be huge. We're going more digital so we _____ meet with _____ people face-to-face."

You're now sprinting to get out of the stupid garage.

"Are you in?" he says.

"Of course! Yes!" you say, finally making it out of the garage and finding a better signal.

"Okay. Put together something and meet in my office in an hour." He hangs up.

You catch your breath. And it hits you. Put together *what*? You're not exactly sure what he said. Your career is riding on this. Did he say:

1. "We're going more digital so we don't have to meet with so many people face-to-face."

2. "We're going more digital, so we have to meet with a lot of people face-to-face."

3. "We're going more digital, so we need to meet with some tech people face-to-face."

Sometimes, you have to do the counterintuitive thing to set the stage for big, brand-minded changes. And, what is more of a counterintuitive than meeting with people face-to-face so that you can go digital?

So, in the real-life case of Partners Federal Credit Union in 2016, the correct answer was, oddly enough… option two, and the CEO was John Janclaes, who we introduced in the last chapter.

Conventional wisdom would dictate that when you are preparing to launch a new digital experience, you'd start with technology vendors. Most leaders would ask to see a demo of the most sleek, sophisticated digital solutions.

John chose to go in the opposite direction. He sought out in-depth conversations with scores of credit union members. John learned what the cast members struggled with, how they fit banking into their demanding jobs in the parks, and how mobile banking could help them.

In the end, Partners launched a digital experience that not only had all of the banking features that members needed (transfers, deposits, bill pay, etc.), but also coupons from local and national merchants, downloadable money management podcasts, and a survey tool for members to provide feedback on the go.[5]

In order to think like a brand, John did the least digital thing there is—talking with real people—to improve the digital experience.

SEARCH FOR SPACE

To better understand what is counterintuitive in banking, let's first define what is intuitive to most bankers. In our experience, there are a few tenets that apply:

- Banks look for ways to make money.

- Banks look for ways to avoid risk.

- Banks see people as customers (not people).

- Banks tend to think in binary terms.

---

[5] https://www.businesswire.com/news/home/20161018005530/en/Kony-Helps-Partners-Federal-Credit-Union-Deliver-Innovative-Mobile-Apps-to-Cast-Members-of-The-Walt-Disney-Company

Don't worry.

We aren't going to launch a diatribe against banks. You don't need to throw everything out.

So let's take these tenets one at a time.

Banks look for ways to make money.

That's fine. It's not a sin to turn a profit. And we'll never tell you that you shouldn't make a profit.

Banks look for ways to avoid risk.

That's understandable. It's not detrimental to avoid unnecessary risk, as long as you aren't labeling new concepts "risky" just because they are uncomfortable.

The next two ingrained concepts in banking, however, are ones that we would like to challenge.

Banks see people as customers (not people).

In order to start seeing customers as complex human beings, think about how most personal relationships begin. Most interpersonal relationships start with getting to know each other. Through sharing musical tastes, hobbies, or the things in life that bring us joy, relationships often begin with finding common ground.

Of course, when someone comes into a credit union to open an account, it might be strange to ask them "Do you like pottery?" instead of "Savings or checking?" We can't prod customers to immediately open up to us. We're strangers.

But, financial institutions are realizing that they can open up first. Banks and credit unions can forge connections by showing that they are human, and then letting customers gravitate toward that humanity.

Rilla Delorier, an independent board director and former Chief Strategy Officer at Umpqua Bank, talked to us about her counterintuitive approach to human-digital banking and the Umpqua Go-To program. The app allows customers to choose their own banker by perusing personal profiles. And, these banker profiles don't just include business skills like "familiar with SBA programs," they include quirky tidbits that help customers see the bank employees as real people.

The power of the Go-To app at Umpqua Bank is that the customer searches for *their* banker, not the other way around. They find you. They choose to become a fan by selecting a banker that shares their mission, values, or interests.

Umpqua banker profiles include relatable details: "Classic cocktail drinker." "Especially gifted napper." "Don't get me started on dogs. I won't stop." "From catching crab on the Oregon coast or hitting up a food truck, I'm always on the go."

A customer won't just walk up to a teller and say, "I'd like to deposit this check and I love mountain biking." But if they see that one of the bankers loves mountain biking, they might select them as their financial expert and chat about biking to break the ice. Customers will begin to open up based on mutual interests.

In the past, selecting your own personal banker was only for the wealthy. But Umpqua made that option available to any bank customer, even someone with only twenty dollars in their account. This is counterintuitive thinking at its best.

And the last ingrained concept in banking that we would like to challenge...

Thinking in binary terms.

When you approach banking with a binary mindset instead of a brand-first mindset, you'll view things as high risk or low risk, profitable or not profitable. But wait, there's more:

- Bankers or advisors

- Digital or brick and mortar

- Personal Coffee or Business Tea (Remember Dan and Jeremy?)

In our experience, a binary mindset often carries over to how banks and credit unions view their customers. Either you're an account holder or you're not. You have a high net worth (at this exact moment) or you don't. You are either a consumer account or a business account.

Binary thinking misses the core of thinking like a brand—the fact that people are multifaceted. If you only see a person as a consumer account, you might miss the fact that her wife owns a lucrative options trading business—and you've now just missed the boat (and the deposits).

These binary terms are the default in many financial institutions today. And so, to think like a brand and do the counterintuitive thing in this environment means finding the opportunities that exist between A and B.

For example, an investment doesn't have to be profitable or not profitable. It all depends on how you view valuation. And in the case of Chime, a company that is not yet profitable, but is valued at $30 billion, it's clear that there is value that is not directly linked to profit.

Between high risk and low risk, there are possibilities. Ventures to be explored. That's where the opportunity for innovation resides. In fact, there's a tremendous amount of space for growth between almost any two choices, and that is the freeing aspect of thinking like a brand.

DOES HISTORY HAVE A PLACE?

As you evaluate how your organization can adapt to a changing world, it's difficult to know how to use (or not use) your bank's celebrated history.

Most banks and credit unions don't know what to do with the traditional elements that have been handed down for generations. Is there still a place for these things as we look to the future?

The intuitive solution for most organizations has been to either stick with bank traditions and resist modernization (if we're making profits, why change?) or…ditch the past and move forward (we can't be weighed down by traditions).

At this point, do we even need to say that's binary thinking?

There's another solution. And it's counterintuitive. In order to innovate, you can look to the past.

Rilla Delorier (former Chief Strategy Officer at Umpqua) reminds us that "the fruits are in the roots." In other words, you shouldn't just look back, but all the way back—to the founding of the organization. If you're not sure how to move forward, you can look at why the bank was originally founded. And when you go back to the beginning, you'll be reminded of the role the institution played in society. You can rediscover your purpose.

Most banks were founded to solve a problem, or fill an unmet need. The way they met that problem was often unique. And, if they landed on a solution that was useful to consumers, they grew. But, that first solution to that first problem often gets lost over the decades (or centuries), so it's essential that the organization gets back in touch with their original Why in order to refresh what they stand for.

Once you get in touch with those origins, you can use that history —that purpose—to guide the new experiences you offer to customers who are underserved or have unmet needs. There are always market opportunities that connect with your organization's original purpose.

Umpqua Bank, in the Pacific Northwest, was founded to serve the unmet needs of lumberjacks in the early 1950s. The working men were getting paid, but, stuck out in a rural logging area, had nowhere to cash their checks. The bank was founded in order to save them a bothersome errand to the nearest town on their precious days off.

Umpqua Bank has grown, of course, and they serve more of the population than just lumberjacks. But, they still tap into their founding principles when deciding what new experiences they should offer their customers.

While Delorier was the Chief Strategy Officer at Umpqua, the Go-To app they rolled (that we mentioned previously) allowed customers to do more without visiting a branch. The solution was different from the original 1950s solution (an app instead of brick and mortar branches), and the customers had changed (retail workers, DoorDash drivers, teachers, etc. instead of lumberjacks), but it still solved the same problem—how to save working folks the time and effort of a trip to the bank.

DON'T BE CUSTOMER FIRST

Yes, you read that correctly. Just hear us out.

We do want you to create new customer experiences that delight. That's important. But it's not either-or—customer first or bank first.

That's binary (not brand) thinking.

A customer-first mindset can impact profitability, which can create tension (more on that later). A bank-first approach makes an emotional connection with the brand more difficult (which reduces growth).

When an organization goes all in on a customer-first mindset, they can overcomplicate their offerings in an attempt to fulfill every need. Sometimes, even when customers are requesting new features, the complexity that comes with those features can detract from the simplicity of the experience that attracted users to the brand in the first place.

If Chime adds wealth and retirement planning services to their app as their users age, they might have to sacrifice the streamlined design that everyone loves.

The counterintuitive belief is that *nobody's first*. And *no one is last*. There is opportunity in the middle—a mutually beneficial outcome that is deeply rewarding to both the bank and customer that strengthens the emotional connection and drives growth.

There is no first, there's only focus.

Now, we'll talk about finding growth opportunities in the middle space.

And, this starts with what not to do.

Don't accept conventional wisdom.

It's limiting.

REAL WORLD EXAMPLE: ELLEVEST

Finding the space in the middle allows you to focus on both (customer and bank) while setting the stage to do some counterintuitive, category-defining work.

Ellevest founder, Sally Krawcheck, started the company in 2014 with a counterintuitive decision, leaving behind a lucrative role and putting her reputation and personal wealth on the line to blast a hole in the conventional wisdom (and even some data sources) that told us women were less likely to invest, plan for wealth, and seek financial advice.

Here is a short list of the binary thinking Ellevest seeks to change:

- That investing isn't some game to be won.

- That investing for impact[6] doesn't have to mean giving up the opportunity for competitive returns.

- That our daughters deserve the same opportunities as our sons. And that when women are stronger financially,[7] we all win.

Krawcheck saw a need—women were tired of being treated like they were dumb with money, didn't earn enough to invest it, or would be too risk averse to invest aggressively. Ellevest stepped in with a clear mission: "To help close the gender money gaps." It's not that Ellevest doesn't offer investment coaching or advice, it's that they do it without binary assumptions.

---

[6] https://www.ellevest.com/magazine/impact-investing/impact-portfolios-win-win

[7] https://www.ellevest.com/magazine/impact-investing/gender-lens-investing

No one is doubting her wisdom now. Ellevest hit the magic $1 billion in Assets Under Management (AUM) at the end of 2020, against the backdrop of COVID-19.

Krawcheck spoke to Forbes Magazine about how she felt about hitting $1 billion AUM: "What I'm particularly proud of is that it happened during a pandemic. And very importantly, at a time when you would think women would be more pulled back, we actually had net positive inflows every single week of the year."

Ellevest did report some impact from the widely reported *she-cession*—where women were more deeply impacted by the economic consequences of COVID-19. For example, their average monthly deposits decreased from $740 to $474, but money kept coming in and, more importantly, money stayed in. This is particularly significant as during the same time period, there was a $241 billion outflow from US equity funds,[8] more than the four next worst years combined.

Ellevest's success is a consequence of rejecting the assumption that women are hard to categorize. They built a multidimensional brand to serve multidimensional customers.

Krawchek rejected black and white thinking, and created a

---

[8] https://www.morningstar.com/articles/1017899/us-fund-flow-records-fell-in-2020

business model that thrived by challenging traditional Wall Street assumptions from the comfort of a gray area that has real growth possibilities.

To successfully operate in this gray area (as you might have guessed), you have to have a brand-first mindset—something Ellevest does incredibly well.

QUIT FIGHTING THE FINTECHS

Nonbanks are identifying clever market niches, and customers are lining up around the digital block to open accounts with them.

But they aren't your competition.

Seriously.

It may feel like they are the competition, especially if you view the financial industry in a binary way (i.e., as having winners and losers).

By playing it safe, by not doing the counterintuitive thing, banks have opened the door to fintechs. Fintechs have filled the void to provide services that people wanted and needed in a financial brand (not institution).

The intuitive response to threat is to compete. Battle these upstarts with better rates, flex your billions in capital, and beat them at the banking game. Don't let them steal your customers.

But that is, wait for it…binary thinking, of course. Today's landscape of banks, credit unions, and fintechs is more nuanced and layered than just winners and losers. There are a multitude of win-win opportunities if we look at the emergence of fintechs through a brand-first lens. Even thinking of a customer as a single unit that can be stolen or lost to the competition is binary thinking. Most people today have multiple accounts across various financial institutions.

Fintechs aren't going to replace banks. But they are gaining trust, which has been the stronghold of chartered financial institutions.[9]

A survey conducted by Ernst and Young Over showed that one-third of consumers now say a fintech is their most trusted financial services brand, compared with 33 percent who name a bank as their most trusted brand, and 12 percent who say they trust a wealth management firm the most.

Fifty-one percent of Gen Z and 49 percent of millennials named a fintech as their most trusted financial brand, a sign that bank thinking might be impacting the relevance of a traditional bank to young people.

---

[9] https://www.ey.com/en_us/nextwave-financial-services/how-financial-institutions-can-win-the-battle-for-trust

Trust in Different Types of US Financial Institutions

BY AGE GROUP

Percentage of Respondents
Trusting Each Type the MOST

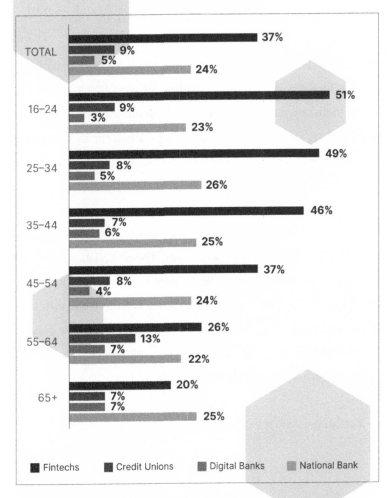

TOTAL
- Fintechs: 37%
- Credit Unions: 9%
- Digital Banks: 5%
- National Bank: 24%

16–24
- Fintechs: 51%
- Credit Unions: 9%
- Digital Banks: 3%
- National Bank: 23%

25–34
- Fintechs: 49%
- Credit Unions: 8%
- Digital Banks: 5%
- National Bank: 26%

35–44
- Fintechs: 46%
- Credit Unions: 7%
- Digital Banks: 6%
- National Bank: 25%

45–54
- Fintechs: 37%
- Credit Unions: 8%
- Digital Banks: 4%
- National Bank: 24%

55–64
- Fintechs: 26%
- Credit Unions: 13%
- Digital Banks: 7%
- National Bank: 22%

65+
- Fintechs: 20%
- Credit Unions: 7%
- Digital Banks: 7%
- National Bank: 25%

■ Fintechs   ■ Credit Unions   ■ Digital Banks   ■ National Bank

Source:https://www.ey.com/en_us/nextwave-financial-services/how-financial-institutions-can-win-the-battle-for-trust

While this chart may look frightening at first glance, there are a few things to remember.

Fintechs are solving problems that banks could solve if they thought more like brands. So, let's take that mindset further, and uncover ways you can bring counterintuitive thinking to the table.

Don't compete: we recommend that you neither compete with nor join the fintechs, but embrace the impact of fintechs. Instead of seeing them only as competition or only as collaborators, view them as a catalyst. The arrival of fintechs has pushed the industry into action, so this is an amazing opportunity to leverage the results of these bold brand experiments.

Look inward to solve outward: Some banks think of fintechs as competitors. Other banks think of fintechs as collaborators. But both camps are thinking about fintechs more than looking internally and thinking about what their organization can offer, and how they can drive innovation. If you worry about all of those new players on the financial landscape infringing on your bank territory, then you're forgetting one fundamental concept:

To a customer, you're not a bank, you're a brand.

REMAKE MOMENTS

Banks have always been there for people during their biggest moments in life. And any bank will tell you—the biggest moment is buying a home.

That is...unless you have a baby.

But there is no "baby loan. That's not a thing...is it?

Banks and credit unions are great at identifying milestones that require financial assistance: going to college, buying a car, buying a home, getting married, and retirement.

But life is more than milestones—it offers plenty of other opportunities for momentum. Banks can step into the space between homeowner, parent, and retiree to create new products and services. What about a gap year account? Or instead of just a home loan, could you offer a green power loan for people who want to live off-grid? How about a second career advisory service?

But this still involves deciding what you think the customer needs. Often, financial institutions think of a product that they would like to sell, and then brainstorm which life moments that product might service. Banks love home mortgages, for instance, because they're low risk and high reward for the organization. So, they go out and see who they can get to sign up for a mortgage.

But, the counterintuitive approach is to let the emotions of consumers lead you to the opportunities.

Instead of building a product or service and then seeing where it could fit, a brand-first organization looks for big, emotional moments in modern consumers' lives, and then designs a new experience around it.

Here's an example: Future Family was created to address the stress and financial hardship created by a modern issue—the in vitro fertilization (IVF) process, which is common today.[10] And with a cost that often reaches over $15,000 per treatment cycle, it can definitely put a strain on finances.[11]

Future Family didn't create a baby loan and then try to find people to buy it. They identified an emotional need that could have a financial solution.

Here's another example: Onward, which offers a seamless way for divorced parents to split payments for their shared child's expenses through an app,[12] redefined inside out thinking as emotion to outcome versus bank to customer.

---

[10] https://www.futurefamily.com/ivf

[11] https://www.forbes.com/health/family/how-much-does-ivf-cost/

[12] https://www.onwardapp.com/

This approach to products and services isn't as counterintuitive as you may think. Remember—people have already been conditioned to go to banks for the big moments in their lives. People naturally look to banks for solutions to the big, daunting challenges they face. Why not take advantage of that dynamic and be there for every big moment...even the nonlinear ones?

Being counterintuitive in a brand context means taking what you already do well and applying it in new ways.

Sometimes, Do the Counterintuitive Thing

1. **Everything builds:** remember, it starts with mindset.

2. **Be open to odd:** doing the counterintuitive things should feel weird; embrace it.

3. **Search for spaces:** brand thinking is not A or B, it's finding the opportunities that exist between the two.

4. **Don't be customer first:** It is not about the customer or the bank winning. It is about both getting the outcomes they need.

5. **Quit fighting fintechs:** Learn from them. Partner with them. You hold the keys to the kingdom through your charter.

6. **Remake moments:** use your abundance of data to innovate new experiences to align with new meaningful moments in your customers' lives.

PRINCIPLE 01

Sometimes, Do the Counterintuitive Thing

REMEMBER

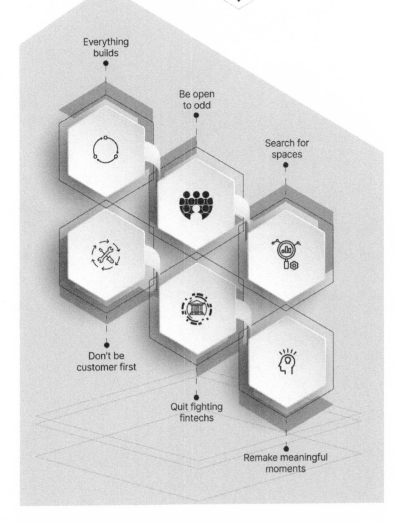

Everything builds

Be open to odd

Search for spaces

Don't be customer first

Quit fighting fintechs

Remake meaningful moments

Chapter 3

PRINCIPLE TWO: EMBRACE TENSION AND CREATE CONTRADICTIONS

"The contradictions are what make human behavior so maddening and yet so fascinating, all at the same time."

—Joan D. Vinge

WE HAVE BEEN PROGRAMMED TO believe that tension is a bad thing. If we feel tense, we get a massage, pour a calming tea, or watch a couple of hours of mindless television. Tension is something we feel the need to escape from.

But tension isn't always a bad thing.

Aren't the strings of a piano tightened to the point of extreme tension? Or the strings of a guitar? What about an artist's canvas stretched tightly over a frame?

When a storyteller uses suspense to build tension, it feels uncomfortable at first. But, without that suspense—that tension—there would be no joy when the hero prevails.

A filmmaker might present the image of a happy child playing on a swing set, but pair it with ominous music. The contradiction between the pleasant visuals and the foreboding score produce a tension. But in a movie theater, we don't run away. We have a belief that things will work out in the end. And the same is true in brand building.

Tension creates energy, and contradictions are not something that always have to be solved. This chapter explores how leaning into discomfort to conquer emotions like fear and avoidance can lead to seismic shifts in thinking, decision making, and business results.

So where does tension come from? Often, it stems from a contradiction.

The story of the evolution of the Umpqua brand is a perfect example.

REAL WORLD EXAMPLE:
UMPQUA BANK

Ray Davis came to South Umpqua Bank in 1994. It was a small town bank with only six locations, but he wanted to make it into something special. Ray hoped to reinvent the branch experience to create emotional connections. So, he went on a walkabout to study the best retail experiences (such as Nordstrom) and best customer service experiences (such as Ritz-Carlton). He then brought those lessons back to his little bank in Roseburg, Oregon.

Instead of hiring a bank designer, they worked with a retail design and marketing specialist to help build their first concept "store."

When the store first opened, people weren't sure what to think. It wasn't uncommon for customers to walk in, look around, then step back outside and read the bank's sign to see whether they had entered the right place.[13]

Ray's team instituted all kinds of new twists on the banking experience. They did away with the teller counters, moving instead to comfortable chairs where customers could chat with a banker side by side, just like you are talking to the concierge in a world class hotel. They gave out little chocolates after each transaction,

---

[13] Raymond P. Davis and Alan Shrader, *Leading for Growth: How Umpqua Bank Got Cool and Created a Culture of Greatness* (San Francisco, CA: Jossey-Bass, 2007).

and served coffee to their guests. But, the most talked about (even twenty-five years later) development was a small station called the Serious About Service Center. This table contained a phone, which rang right to Ray's desk. Employees called it the "Ray Phone."

At first, Ray thought it would just be a way for people in the community to get to know him. But by 1999, he had become the CEO of Umpqua Holdings Corporation, and the company was growing. And as the company grew, Ray Davis did something even more counterintuitive.

He put Ray Phones in every store. And, all of the phones still rang directly to the CEO's office.

How did Ray know that giving direct access to 500,000 people would build brand value?

He didn't.

But, he wanted to build a brand that would better serve his customers, so he leaned into contradiction and embraced tension. He did something that most institutions actively try to prevent—one-to-one conversation. (Remember Dan, the grilled cheese specialist in our Starbucks story?)

Ray wanted customers to know that they were the most important part of the bank. Every one of them had a direct line to the CEO so that he could either personally solve their issue, or put Umpqua's resources behind it.

The Ray Phone calls were often feedback about employees, or simply checking to see if he really did answer, but every now and then a customer had a real problem, like: "My employer wrote my paycheck from an Umpqua account, but the tellers won't let me cash it because I don't bank here." And when a call like that reached the CEO, it forced everyone—from top to bottom—to rethink the policy, and sometimes question why it was a policy at all.

Tension can be useful.

Giving over 500,000 customers[14] direct access to a CEO is not standard practice, but sometimes, in order to think more like a brand and less like a bank, you have to do the counterintuitive thing.

The fear of organizational change comes from that pang of tension in the beginning. So brace yourself for that feeling. It's not going to feel great initially. But that fear and discomfort is a barometer of the power of change.

Lean in. There are breakthroughs for your brand on the other side.

---

[14] Umpqua Bank 2020 ESG Report

MODERNIZE THE ROLES

To affect changes with a significant external impact, some big internal changes have to be made.

A brand-first mindset will force you to question the traditional organizational chart, and elevate customer-centered roles to positions of greater power. Banks typically have an EVP of business banking, an EVP of retail banking, an EVP of corporate and investment banking, an EVP of risk management, and so on.

Remember Vincent Stanley, Patagonia's Director of Philosophy?

But, what if we flipped the organizational structure so that your bank or credit union had a fully empowered EVP of digital innovation? Wouldn't they make a very different set of decisions than an EVP of retail lending or an EVP of investment banking? To think like brands, more decision-making authority is needed for customer and experience focused roles.

What if we took the subject matter experts and gave them power? And then took the EVPs with all the power and made them subject matter experts?

We're not saying to fire the EVP of business banking who has forty years of experience. That experience is valuable. The organization should still come to them for advice on complex commercial situations. But, we are saying that the internal structure of financial institutions needs a refresh.

Can you feel the tension? Have we created a contradiction?

Good.

SIMPLE VERSUS COMPLEX

Have you ever heard a coworker say, "Let's make our website more complicated"?

Probably not.

No one sets out to make the banking experience more complicated or confusing. But year after year, new option after new option, a bank's value proposition can become muddled.

Here's an experiment we'd like you to try:

Pick a major national bank and take a look at their homepage. When you explore all the drop-down menus on that page (from personal, to small business, to commercial banking; from checking, to savings, to money market accounts; from credit card options, to types of auto, home, and business loans) how many links are there to choose from on that page?

Now go to Chime's website. How does their website compare? What about their mobile app? Is it simpler than the major national bank?

There is a contradiction in the financial world between offering the customer more options and keeping it simple, and between profitability and valuation. It is the tension between being everything to everyone, which is what the large banks try to do, and a highly targeted minimalist offering, which is what most of the new fintech and de novo banks are doing.

Corey LeBlanc, Co-founder of Locality Bank, believes that Chime does an excellent job of defining who they are and what they can provide. They put that message in front of the customer as much as they possibly can, and it resonates. To illustrate this, LeBlanc points to a conversation he had with an Uber driver. "He can't tell me anything Chime does from an account perspective," LeBlanc said, "but he knows Chime can give him an account, and knows it will be helpful for him. And that's all he needs to know."

There's an old saying in sales: "Stop when you get to yes." It's a concept that the new fintechs seem to understand. Chime offers just enough features to get people to sign up. And then they stop.

Traditional banks, however, seem to have a hard time with this concept. They keep building and building until they build beyond what's useful. When faced with the tension between complexity and simplicity, banks inadvertently favor complexity in an effort to offer everything to everyone. "People need to be able to do this, and do this, and do this. And they need to do it all on the go." They make banking harder than it needs to be. Meanwhile, the brands that are successful in today's financial landscape (the brands that we all wish we were) employ only the most simple forms of banking. In many cases, they are little more than just a checking account.

In co-founding a new bank, LeBlanc has embraced the tension between complexity and simplicity, and when faced with that tension, he leaned into simplicity. Focusing only on business banking in one geographic region (South Florida), Locality Bank parallels the broader industry movement towards narrower, more specialized banking.

YOU THINK YOU KNOW THE CUSTOMER

One area of consistent tension in the financial world is the mission to know the customer. And it's true…bankers know a lot about their customers at points in time, but people change moment to moment, and this creates a substantial amount of tension, especially when you realize *you will never stop getting to know your customer.*

You can't get to know your customer by simply asking them what they want, because they often can't articulate exactly what they want. Although there is no simple shortcut to truly knowing the customer, it is possible to embrace that tension.

John Janclaes describes how he manages this tension with an approach called Always on Strategy. Although it isn't a consistently comfortable exercise, Janclaes seeks to know the customer better through "widening the aperture of your vision of what's coming in the world." In other words, he tries to keep one eye on the horizon. If he can spot innovations that are coming—in other areas of the financial industry or even in nonbanking industries—he can predict what his customers will want before they even know about it. If you can see the change coming, you may not know where to place it on the timeline, but you know customers are going to want it sooner or later.

The onus is on us to innovate. We can't expect the customer to do our innovation for us. What we can do is think of new ways to know our customers better, and invent ways for them to discover what they need and want.

For an applicable example, let's look at the Royal Bank of Scotland (RBS). Several years ago, the bank allowed a team of researchers to run a bold experiment. After closing time one day, the researchers invited a group of customers to take over a branch of the bank. (Can you feel the tension?)

Locked in the branch from 4 p.m. to 8 p.m. with the research team, the customers were allowed to run the branch, and were asked to place sticky notes on all of the things they would change. They were given no limitations on their suggestions (even if it meant completely scrapping an existing branch feature and starting all over again). The brilliance of this research experiment is that it flipped the usual equation and created a contradiction. Instead of putting themselves in the customer's shoes, RBS instead placed the customer in the bank employee's shoes. It produced great research insights, but also indirectly gave the customer a hand in shaping the future strategy of the bank.

In order for that project to take place, the bank leadership had to embrace a considerable amount of tension. They not only had to let the customers into the bank after hours (yikes), but also had to let the customers rethink things that had taken decades to build. The bank allowed fresh pairs of eyes to look at what they were doing every day. That took guts. And it epitomizes the process of embracing tension and thinking of creative new approaches to getting to know your customers.

TEST, LEARN, AND
MOVE ON

Justin Dunn, who scored a major success at WSFS Bank with his WissFiss rebranding campaign, admits that other campaigns did not go nearly as well.

And he was cool with that.

Dunn's way of embracing tension is to face, head-on, the fear of failure. He conceded that WSFS has had campaigns that "have just bombed" from an acquisition standpoint, yielding little to no growth. But the bank is not afraid to fail. And if they do fail, they prefer to fail fast.

"In our recap, as long as we're focused on our learnings and take-aways, and we know what to do differently next time, it's supported," Dunn said. WSFS Bank, as an organization, knows that they're not going to get it right every single time. So not only is Dunn accepting of the occasional failure, he has fostered a culture at the bank that accepts it as well.

Before we move on, we should be clear on one point: no one wants to fail. So it may be imprecise to say it's best to go ahead and fail fast. In fact, once you put the label of *failure* on a project, it can hinder learning from the experience. A more positive spin on the concept is *test and learn*. You're not failing. You're learning.

The concept of test and learn is yet another aspect of the brand mindset. Remember the barriers to growth question? Exactly... there aren't any. There is a built-in positivity to the brand mindset. A feeling that anything is possible if the brand mindset is right. In keeping with that, "there is no failure, just testing and learning" is an important part of the brand mindset with each new project.

So test, learn, and move on.

Embrace Tension and Create Contradictions

1. **Beautiful brands are born from tension:** Embrace it. If it feels uncomfortable, it's probably a breakthrough.

2. **Modernize your roles:** give customer and experience focused roles decision-making authority and watch innovation happen.

3. **Keep it simple:** Subtract complexity. Don't be everything to everyone. Do a few unique things brilliantly.

4. **Stop when you get to yes:** Do what it takes to win a customer and make them profitable. It's what Chime does, and it's worth $40 billion.

5. **Test, learn, and move on:** Failure is not to be feared. Remember there are no barriers to growth, only opportunities not taken.

PRINCIPLE 02

Embrace Tension and Create Contradictions

REMEMBER

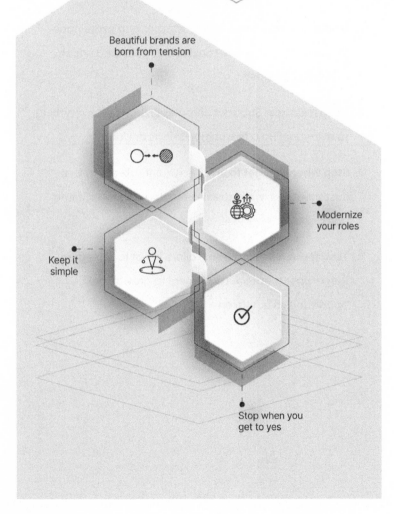

Beautiful brands are born from tension

Modernize your roles

Keep it simple

Stop when you get to yes

Chapter 4

PRINCIPLE THREE: CUE THE REMIX

"If you think you have to reimagine everything in the world, good luck."

—Corey LeBlanc, Co-Founder, Locality Bank

THERE'S A DANGEROUS TEMPTATION when trying to change to a brand first mindset—the urge to throw everything out to make wholesale changes: "Everything old out. Everything new in."

Resist that temptation.

When you throw everything out and start at zero, you lose momentum on the aspects of your strategy that were actually working.

Instead, start small—as in, make your decisions smaller—and cue the remix.

We want you to use the raw materials available in your organization to create a "remix" that connects with customers' needs. If you take the time to examine your institution, you'll see that you already have plenty of valuable elements (i.e., talent, technology, ideas, etc.) that you can remix and use in fresh, exciting ways.

And if you really want to embrace remixing, you should adopt a broader definition of what your remix ingredient are.

Nothing is off limits.

The name of your bank or credit union, the way the technology works, anything is fair game. Forget all of the unspoken rules regarding what you can't touch. Remix means redefining what materials are available to you as you start thinking more like a brand.

Mindset is, of course, a key to remixing. You have to have a brand-first mindset and be willing to embrace tension, because often the fresh ideas are within silos. Leaning into contradictions and tension can lead to game-changing innovation. And, the great news is that you don't need to start from scratch!

For example, many banks now offer a round up feature to retail customers that allows them to round up every purchase to the nearest dollar, and automatically transfer the change to their savings account. It's the digital version of a piggy bank. But if you suggest to most bankers that they should offer this to small business owners (or even large business accounts), they are confused.

"Wait...what? But that's for consumers..." (That would be something our Starbucks friends, Dan and Jeremy, would say.)

But if you lean into that contradiction, you'll realize that a round up doesn't have to exist in just one part of the bank. Whether a customer is rounding up for personal savings or rounding up for their business, what difference does it make? You already have the technology. You already have the marketing. You have the raw materials...you can remix and offer a round up to entrepreneurs or eighteen-wheeler drivers who need to save for taxes.

A remix involves putting things together in a way that may not seem comfortable at first. You're combining two things that would traditionally not coexist, but together could form something original and innovative.

Remixing new experiences for the financial consumer is all about reimagining what a bank or credit union does, and what it could possibly do. Yes, it's a bank, but what else could it be? Yes, it's a credit union smartphone app, but what else could it be? Yes, it's a loan application, but what else could it be?

Could the smartphone app not only check the customer's balance, but also send invoices to their clients? Could the loan application be presented as an invitation—to which the customer fills out an RSVP instead of a loan form? Could your wealth managers also be wealth Sherpas who can guide lower-income customers toward wealth?

Imagine the outcomes that the consumer is seeking—less hassle, less stress, prosperity, life balance, etc. And then, imagine unconventional ways that your organization could help them reach those outcomes.

And—spoiler alert—it will probably have nothing to do with how they check their balance or the furniture in your lobby.

REAL WORLD EXAMPLE: GIG WORKERS

An Uber driver walks into a bank.

No, this is not the beginning of a bad joke. But it is a situation that might call for a remix of existing products and services.

Consider the Uber driver's experience when entering a bank or credit union to open a new account. What is the first question the driver is likely to encounter? "Will this be a personal or business account?" And the driver might be stumped. "Um…," she says, staring at the teller for an uncomfortably long time. She can't make it past the first question, because Uber drivers don't neatly fall into one category.

To a bank, the majority of gig workers will look like normal retail banking customers. They won't look like a business, but for all intents and purposes, they are. They're freelancers, and many of them have multiple income sources (many Uber drivers also drive for Lyft, for example). They're individual gig workers, but are actually closer to being small businesses.

So, let's say you set out to create a new bank that will accommodate these gig workers—customers who have personal financial needs, but also more businesslike needs. You'll need the concept of remixing.

You have plenty of raw material within your institution that you can remix—it's simply seeing what you have at your disposal and remixing its use in a different way.

So for your new bank for gig workers, you would invent an entirely different set of customer experiences than if you were launching a traditional retail or a traditional small-business bank, because in those traditional models, the gig workers would fall in the hole between the two of them. To remix existing ideas and create a new freelancer account, you would have to embrace the tension and create a contradiction.

This new account is not a retail account or a business account. It's both. And neither. (Head explodes.) It's okay to feel uncomfortable. This new account has some elements of personal banking and some elements of business banking. It's a remix from the best of both worlds.

So, how do you come up with more "remix" ideas for your bank or credit union? Well...(and you can probably see this coming)...you have to think more like a brand.

If you want to reexamine what your retail customers' needs might be and come up with some great remixes, it's necessary to get away from the standard questions like, "Do they need a better mortgage rate?" or "Do they need a mobile app?" Those are things that everyone needs. Try thinking about a segment within that retail population, and you'll start to discover really different needs. You can then mesh together the main functions of a business bank and the main functions of a retail bank and create something new and unique. Something that creates an emotional connection and real value.

That is brand thinking.

NONBANKS CRASH THE PARTY

Sometimes, to get a clear view of these principles in action, it helps to step outside the banking industry and study well-known brands in other business sectors.

In fact, some of the clearest examples of brand-first banking have come from nonbanks.

Imagine if you could combine the empowered, customer-centric call center of Zappos with the passion driven, save-the-planet mission of Aspiration. What if a company had a purpose based on shared values with their clients, but also had a legendary level of customer care?

Or what if you could combine Daylight with Ritz-Carlton? Imagine the mission driven, empowering values of Daylight mixed with the anything-to-deliver-a-great-experience service of Ritz-Carlton.

If you could do a remix and use a Zappos-type approach to rewrite the banking forms at the Big Five banks, just think what could happen across our industry!

Keeping the same lens of nonbanks, let's look at Starbucks. With the Starbucks app, you can send money to a friend who just paid for your coffee. That's a peer-to-peer payment, and it used to be solidly in the dominion of banks and financial services companies.

But Starbucks, thinking like a brand, decided to add the option to their app because it makes life easier for their consumers. It is truly a remix because the app already existed, and customers were already storing balances in the app. Starbucks needed only to remix the raw materials to find a new solution for its customers.

These cases of embedded finance, or banking as a service, are becoming more and more common across a wide spectrum of brands. Even that little add-on service that you see when paying for an online purchase, "Would you like to split this into four payments?" is an example of embedded finance. And some companies, like Home Depot, have taken this concept to another level.

If you are a professional contractor at Home Depot, you can do all of your ordering, pay your invoices, borrow money, and use a credit card—all without leaving the brand. Credit card perks such as sixty days interest free (or six months on larger purchases) are actually banking propositions disguised as a retail benefit. And these extra services from Home Depot go a long way in building and cementing (no pun intended) their relationship with this niche audience.

Home Depot created a contradiction—doing your banking with a hardware store—and has remixed the services that they offer to make that a reality. It may have been uncomfortable in the beginning, but the brand loyalty they created has translated into solid returns (and an enviable eighteenth spot on the Forbes 500).

KEY TAKEAWAYS

Cue the Remix

1. **Make your decisions smaller:** take your strengths and make them even uniquely stronger.

2. **Good things can happen in silos, great things happen when you break them down:** if something valuable is operating in a silo, set it free and make it a power ingredient in the remix.

3. **Don't ask what can we do, ask what could we do:** Change the question to change the mindset. Nothing is off limits.

4. **Make your financial products into brand experiences:** seamlessly integrated into an existing brand experience.

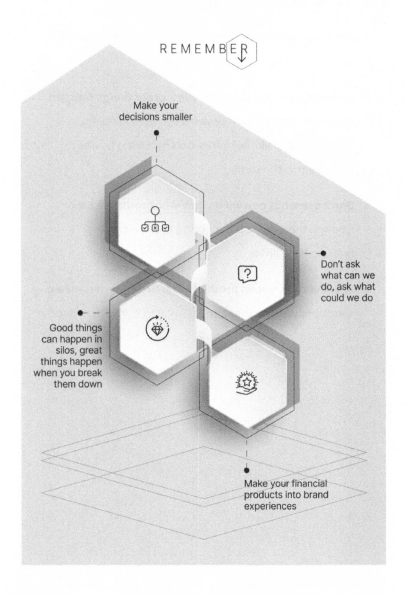

PRINCIPLE 03

Cue the Remix

REMEMBER

Make your
decisions smaller

Don't ask
what can we
do, ask what
could we do

Good things
can happen in
silos, great
things happen
when you break
them down

Make your financial
products into brand
experiences

Chapter 5

PRINCIPLE FOUR: REMEMBER, PRODUCT ISN'T WHAT IT USED TO BE

"Don't find customers for your products, find products for your customers."

—Seth Godin

THIS IS A BIG DAY for Joe Martinez.

Today is the day he officially starts his own business. After fifteen years of working for restaurants and caterers, he's finally ready to launch his own café. He already put a deposit on a great space in an up-and-coming neighborhood—the kind of neighborhood with students and artists pouring in, and renovations on every block. Joe is excited for two reasons: his food is great, and students and artists can't cook.

Joe doesn't know a lot about being an entrepreneur, but he knows that he's going to need a small business account. He googles small business banking and clicks on Megabank.com.

Their homepage provides more options than answers, with messaging like:

ONLINE BONUS! $200 cash back with no annual fee. Unlimited 1.5% cash back on purchases. OR: ONLINE BONUS 25,000 travel rewards. No annual fee and unlimited 1.5 bonus points for each dollar spent. OR: 0% APR for eighteen months—

Wait—these are credit cards. Joe navigates to the small business page.

EARN 1.5% CASHBACK ON PURCHASES FOR YOUR BUSINESS! And $750 bonus cash or 75,000 rewards points toward hotel stays...Hotel stays? Will I even...LEARN ABOUT 2020 AND 2021 PPP LOAN FORGIVENESS! Uh...I just need...EXPLORE AN ALL-IN-ONE BUSINESS CHECKING SOLUTION! Only $25/month or $0/month. Learn how to avoid the fee...Do I need checking? Do people still write checks?

Joe goes back to Google, and this time he finds Square. On the homepage he clicks on Products—Banking. And is greeted with…

"Your payments, banking, and cash flow. Working as one."

There's a Get Started button! He clicks on Business Types—Food and Beverage—Fast Casual. And it's all there: options for ringing up customers, the orders automatically tied to the kitchen, tied to his account, tied to QuickBooks, and with a support team that will help him set it up.

He scrolls through the Square website, which is filled with other small business owners chasing their dreams.[15] Joe isn't looking for a product, he's looking for a banking partner that understands his vision—and he found that partner in Square, through their online experience.

Yes, products are critical. You can't run a bank if you don't have credit cards, checking accounts, savings accounts, or loans. But, there are only so many ways a customer can check their balance.

Product is not brand. A product is a delivery mechanism.

---

[15] https://squareup.com/us/en

Banks can't exclusively lean on products or technology to stand out like they used to. Although products are critical, banks need a brand-first mindset to create the value that the product delivers.

It's how you deliver your brand and experience, not how you define it.

PRODUCT IS
NOT A LANGUAGE

Products and features are not a stand in for clear, relatable language.

If you're just talking about product, then you're staying in bank language. You're not using brand language. Brand language is about the challenges, opportunities, and outcomes in everyday life and business.

For example, where bank language would tout "2% cashback on all purchases!" brand language will point out, "Average cashback of $450 a year. That could be a car payment!" Brands put their benefits in the language of the customer.

Here are a few other examples of common bank language versus your customer's language.

Bank Language	Customer Language
Treasury Management	Managing cash flow
Positive Pay	Preventing check fraud
Payables	How I pay people
Receivables	How I get paid
ACH Cash Management	Paying and getting paid digitally
Merchant Services	Allowing my customers to pay by card
Lockbox	Let the bank capture my customer check payments and make the deposits

If you look at the language you're currently using through the lens of customer experience, we're willing to bet there is room for improvement and, more importantly, help set the mindset for brand-first thinking.

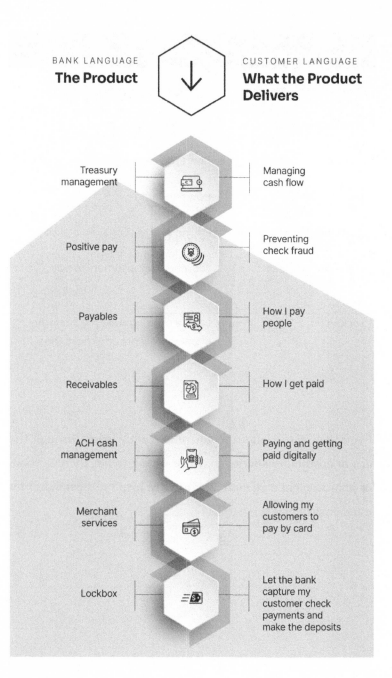

BANK LANGUAGE
The Product

CUSTOMER LANGUAGE
What the Product Delivers

Treasury management — Managing cash flow

Positive pay — Preventing check fraud

Payables — How I pay people

Receivables — How I get paid

ACH cash management — Paying and getting paid digitally

Merchant services — Allowing my customers to pay by card

Lockbox — Let the bank capture my customer check payments and make the deposits

THINK LIKE A BRAND, NOT A BANK

FYI: LOYALTY IS NOT WHAT
IT USED TO BE EITHER

With the exception of the new insurance company, Lemonade, there has been very little innovation in the world of product loyalty in recent years. Lemonade, to their credit, found a way to combine loyalty with a mission-based brand.

Meanwhile, companies that focus on the old "points make prizes" model of loyalty are struggling to build deep connections. These companies are now realizing that their customers are not loyal to them, they're loyal to that free trip to Hawaii they get when they cash in their points.

Most loyalty programs are hoping to hold on to the customers they have. But if your dream as an organization is to not shrink," you need to dream bigger.

Ideally, you should never have to pay customers to stay or to trust you with their money. It is no longer enough to keep people only with points, cashback, or free tickets.

On the other hand, creating a mutual value equation allows you to form a deeper bond that drives life long customer value.

In 2019, Gallup conducted a retail banking study with over 24,000 respondents across every consumer banking segment—retail, insurance, and wealth management. They found that customers who strongly agreed with four or more of the statements below had substantially higher lifetime value:

- Helps me reach my financial goals.

- Understands my financial situation.

- Makes it easy for me to manage my finances.

- Helps me make better financial decisions.

- Looks out for my financial wellbeing.

- Offers solutions to meet my financial needs.

- Puts my financial wellbeing ahead of the interests of the bank.

- Has my best interests at heart.

The study showed that 77 percent of the respondents who strongly agreed with at least four of these statements felt engaged with their bank. And if you remember from Chapter 1, engaged customers deliver 35 percent more revenue than unengaged ones. Perhaps most significantly, the engaged customers in the study entrusted their banks with a higher share of wallet. In fact, one-fifth of them entrusted their banks with 80 percent to 100 percent of their total investable assets.

Engaged customers aren't just loyal to a product or prize, they are loyal to the brand. And they won't just stick around—they'll advocate for you. They'll tell their friends and neighbors. Creating advocacy is far more efficient and cost effective than performing loyalty program maintenance.

PRODUCT IS A VEHICLE FOR VALUE

When product is the offer to customers, you're giving product more importance than the general public, which means there isn't an aligned view of value.

For example, a banker thinks, "How could anyone turn away 0 percent interest?" But, these types of promotions are using product to stand in for brand power. Remember, product is most useful as a delivery mechanism for shared value.

Traditionally, banks leverage offers to acquire customers, but using product alone will not create sustained growth. It's subtle, but a credit card rate is less important than what the credit card allows customers to do. When you deliver what the customer values—a concert, a flight, starting a side hustle—you go beyond the transactional to the meaningful.

A brand-first mindset creates a contextual experience for consumers. A prime example is the famous "Priceless" campaign launched by MasterCard in 1997.[16]

One of the first ads in the campaign featured a father taking a son to a baseball game, with a voiceover narrating the expenses involved. "Two tickets...twenty-eight dollars. Two hot dogs, two popcorns, and two sodas...eighteen dollars. One autographed baseball...forty-five dollars. Real conversation with eleven-year-old son...priceless. There are some things money can't buy. For everything else, there's MasterCard."

The ad focused on the experiences the MasterCard product makes possible. And it worked brilliantly (remember the value of the Mastercard brand alone is $112 billion).

Back in Chapter 1, we talked about making sure that your organization doesn't view brand as something soft and fluffy. We discussed that a strong brand has concrete value in dollars and cents. So, taking a brand-first mindset with a product doesn't mean being abstract. It isn't altruistic or unrelated to profitability. This approach has the same foundation as traditional approaches (product), but the brand-first mindset focuses on creating shared value.

---

[16] https://www.marketingweek.com/mastercard-priceless-campaign/

MISSION
AS PRODUCT

We can care about something without putting any effort into it. We can care about pre-K education ("Of course I support pre-K!"), but skip the bake sale the local nursery school is holding. We can care about social justice, but limit our activism to the "like" button on social media.

Mission, on the other hand, is intentional and, with a brand-first mindset firmly in place, mission can be your product.

When your mission is your product, interest doesn't end with "I care." You're constantly dreaming up new experiences that could improve your customers' lives.

You might care about having a cleaner city, but that doesn't mean it's your mission to clean it up.

A true customer obsession is often mission driven. You find the mission that inspires your ideal customer, rather than creating a mission to attract certain customers. You find what drives them. And then, you obsess over that mission.

REAL WORLD EXAMPLE: STUDIO BANK

Nashville is the capital of country music with attractions like the Grand Ole Opry House and the Country Music Hall of Fame. It is also home to tens of thousands of working musicians, artists, and creators who are drawn to the plentiful job opportunities and the camaraderie of a growing community of artists.

In 2018, Studio Bank was the first de novo bank to open in Nashville in more than ten years, and it quickly drew local support. Aaron Dorn, President and CEO, surpassed his capital raise goal of $40 million, and the bank attracted over 85 percent of local investors.

"We want to be a bank for Nashville's creators," Dorn said. "And I'm not saying creatives because that could be exclusive. It's creators…people who are creating a better healthcare system, people conceiving of something and trying to go out and make it happen, and they need capital to do that…And they need a place to safeguard the fruit of their creativity in a way that is well-managed and safely held. That's what a bank does."

Inspired by the mission of the artists they serve, Studio Bank created an incredible product: a remix of modern technology and community mission.

Its success and record growth can be ascribed to the way Studio offers the best of both worlds. It provides customers with the combination of a large bank's up-to-date technology and seamless user experience with a local bank's community-centric focus.

Studio Bank also remixed digital first with a brick and mortar presence just minutes away from the energetic activity of Broadway. If you stop by Studio, you will be welcomed with an employee-curated Spotify playlist and a bright mural of their mascot, the French Bulldog, done by a local Nashville artist.

Studio is a welcoming place for any type of creator (builders, entrepreneurs, songwriters, coders, etc.). The bank wants to help improve the financial wellness of creators so they can hone their craft, and focus on creativity. A great example is the Studio Women's Collective, a group that connects more than 600 female leaders and entrepreneurs in the Nashville area. Members gather monthly, collaborate on projects, and network across various industries.

They also host community events. For example, during Black History Month, they hosted a tour of the National Museum of African American Music, and heard from the CEO of a women run, ethical fashion brand.

They also hosted local children for Financial Literacy Month. Local kids toured the vault, learned how money is made, and participated in financial education activities. Studio's involvement in the community creates a more informed and financially confident future for Nashville.

Studio Bank is a purpose-driven bank. Its sole focus is not on returning profit but on authentic actions and serving the creative community.

But here is the good news, behind Studio's brand and mission sits a well-run bank. By following their mission, they are selling products—not the other way round. And—you guessed it—this brand thinking is driving returns.

Studio Bank finished 2020, only its second full calendar year in business, and in the middle of a global pandemic, with a profit of $815,000, after being in the green every month since June.

They ended 2020 with $435 million in assets and about $260 million in net loans. Those numbers were up 93 percent and 61 percent, respectively, from the figures of twelve months earlier, and they are 15 percent ahead of their original growth plan.

Mission sells.

WARNING! A MISSION STATEMENT IS NOT A MISSION

Let's play a game.

Can you name each major bank by its mission or vision statement?

1. "To satisfy our customers' financial needs and help them succeed financially."

2. "To serve as a trusted partner to our clients by responsibly providing financial services that enable growth and economic progress."

3. "To change banking for good by bringing humanity, ingenuity and simplicity to banking."

4. "For more than 160 years, we have been committed to providing our clients with great service and powerful financial expertise to help them meet their financial goals."

What if we made it a matching game? Would that help? Try to match these major banks with their mission or vision statement above: Capital One[17], Citigroup[18], PNC Financial[19], and Wells Fargo.[20]

How's it coming?

---

17 https://www.capitalone.com/about/corporate-information/our-company/

18 https://www.citigroup.com/citi/about/mission-and-value-proposition.html

19 https://www.pnc.com/en/about-pnc.html

20 https://www.wellsfargojobs.com/about-us

Now let's look at two more statements from smaller, niche banks.

1. "A digital mobile banking experience made for Black and Latino customers."

2. "_____ helps our customers spend, save, and invest with a conscience so you can make money while making the world a better place."

Can you spot which one is Greenwood?[21] And which one is Aspiration?[22]

All banks and credit unions have some sort of mission statement. But a mission statement is not a mission. A mission statement usually ties into the default setting—caring. The tone of a mission statement often expresses that the organization cares about the people they serve. "We're here to serve the community, the hard-working people of (insert state, county, or city here)." But a mission is very, very different.

The issue with these broad mission statements becomes apparent when you try to apply them. They're simply too general. If your mission is, "To serve people of Napa Valley," exactly how will you do that? And why do you do that? When we apply the "who, what,

---

[21] https://www.aspiration.com/who-we-are/

[22] https://bankgreenwood.com/

when, where, why, and how" to an institution's mission statement, we usually discover that it is not tied to a passionate mission.

"Who is your mission for?"

"The people of Napa Valley."

"What is your mission?"

"To, uh…serve them."

"When?"

"From 9:00 to 5:00 Monday through Friday and from 8:30 to noon on Saturdays."

"Where do you carry out this mission? Digitally? In person?"

"Wherever they are, I guess."

"Why?"

"Because, um…we're the bank on main street?"

"How do you serve them?"

"We have great rates."

Do you think people will line up around the block for that mission?

We doubt it.

REAL WORLD EXAMPLE: CHASE BANK AND DAYLIGHT

For a demonstration of the difference between a mission statement and a mission, you need only to compare Chase Bank and Daylight.

Daylight is a new digital banking experience for the LGBTQ+ community. They explain their mission like this: "Our community has $1 trillion spending power in the US and yet 53 percent of LGBTQ+ people constantly struggle to maintain regular savings. That's high-key unacceptable. We're done letting the system ignore us. We're building Daylight around our unique needs: different timelines, different kinds of families, different goals, and different futures."

They make it quite clear that this is personal to them. "We were founded by queer millennials to solve problems we've experienced already. We've been there, so we get it. For Daylight, it's more than just slapping a rainbow on a card. It's about personal wins, set and met goals, and the success of the community around us." That is their mission.[23]

---

[23] https://www.joindaylight.com/who-we-are

THINK LIKE A BRAND, NOT A BANK

Chase Bank also makes their position clear. "We believe in, and are committed to, a culture of respect, equity and inclusion. Together, we are working across the entire firm—being intentional to strengthen our inclusive environment where our employees, customers and partners feel welcomed and valued in the communities where we do business."[24] They even have an Office of LGBT+ Affairs which "partners closely with stakeholders across the firm to promote intersectionality and leverage our combined resources to deliver equity and inclusion for LGBT+ employees, clients, partners and communities, worldwide."[25] The Human Rights Campaign Foundation has recognized Chase for having an outstanding record of inclusive hiring practices.[26]

At Daylight, they will honor the name that you choose to be called, even if it's different from the name on your ID card. They have tools that allow their customers to see how queer friendly their spending is (and offering "Up to 10 percent cash back for spending at Queer bars and LGBTQ+ allied businesses"). And, they offer a support community for specific LGBTQ+ needs, such as saving up for a transition.

So, which one is driven by a mission statement, and which one is driven by an obsessive mission to serve a specific customer segment?

---

[24] https://www.jpmorganchase.com/about/people-culture/diversity-and-inclusion

[25] https://www.jpmorganchase.com/impact/people/lgbt-plus-affairs

[26] https://www.hrc.org/resources/best-places-to-work-for-lgbtq-equality-2022

There's a limit to mission statements. But there's no limit to a mission.

MAKING PRODUCT WHAT
IT SHOULD BE

If you want to form a meaningful relationship with an environmentalist, you don't focus on finding the environmentalist, you obsess over the environment. If you want to click with an artist, you obsess over the arts. You're not obsessing about a person. You're obsessing over the thing that inspires the person—the thing they connect with.

When you share a common vision with a customer, you'll both be focused on the same thing. And that's what forms a strong bond.

And these inspired, mission-as-product financial organizations are already starting to pop up.

Aspiration is a digital bank that is focused on a greener planet (not just environmentally conscious people). They refuse to invest in oil funds and other financial instruments that could harm the environment.

Greenwood is a bank that's committed to serving the breadth of Black and Latinx communities, not just creating a product for these communities. Inspired by the history of the Greenwood District of Tulsa, Oklahoma, this new digital bank is on a mission to circulate the money earned by thriving Black and Latinx entrepreneurs back into their own communities.[27]

Dolly Parton's Imagination Library is a foundation with a mission to provide free books to any kid who wants one. The product is not books, it's to foster a love of reading. And it has resonated with people who share the same goal. Powered by donations, they've given out more than 172 million books in five countries.[28]

Finally, a product doesn't have to take itself too seriously. Three entrepreneurs launched a toilet paper subscription service with a mission of improving world health by building toilets in the developing world. The name of the company says it all: Who Gives A Crap.[29]

Product has potential, but it needs to be reimagined through the lens of missions that matter.

---

[27] https://bankgreenwood.com/

[28] https://imaginationlibrary.com/

[29] https://us.whogivesacrap.org/

BACK TO BASICS: SHARED UNIT OF VALUE

Rates matter. Offers matter. Combining these with outcomes that matter to the customer is what creates a shared unit of value.

And with a shared unit of value, you create an emotional connection that benefits both parties.

Remember, great brands get great returns every time. Brands that create emotional connections transcend business models and technology, creating an obsession.

The Good Kind of Obsession

A healthy obsession is a two-way street. Both the business and the customer agree on a common obsession (i.e., that shared unit of value). When obsession is mutually agreed upon, it's not a stalker situation. It's a marriage.

A healthy obsession also requires a certain amount of listening. By paying attention to your customers, you ensure that the obsession remains mutual.

Positive obsessions tend to benefit the larger community. If you're obsessed with cleaning up city parks, no one will stop you, because the community shares your mission. Olympians, musicians, artists, and inventors are all obsessive. But they create art, music, inventions, and thrilling sports moments that benefit the community.

Healthy obsessions: anything that makes the world a better place.

How do you know when the obsession is healthy? When your customers are advocating for you in the community without being asked. If consumers are evangelizing on your behalf, you know the relationship is mutual.

When a bank focuses on the features and functionality of their product instead of the outcomes (choice, freedom, time with your son at a ballgame), they actually devalue their product. It's the outcome for the customer that has universal value.

Let's take a moment to acknowledge that obsession can be a loaded word. It may bring to mind stalkers, serial killers, and K-pop fans. For a certain generation, the movie *Single White Female* may come to mind.

These are creepy obsessions.

And the defining characteristic of creepy obsessions is the fact that they are one way. In other words, one party is obsessed, while the other party is not. It's like those ads that follow you, popping up on every website as you surf the internet, until you scream, "Damn you! Stop following me! I don't want the striped patio umbrella!" (Or maybe that's just us?)

An example of a creepy obsession would be a credit union employee scrolling through Facebook looking for potential customers. "Hey, Tonya! I see that you love beagles! Me too! Come by my office on Monday, and I'll show you some photos of my dog and sign you up for a checking account!"

The focus must be on shared commitment and value.

Fintechs Focus on Shared Value

Most financial institutions have the same or better technology than fintechs.

Look at Acorns, for example. Their primary product is a round up feature. Users can round up every purchase, and the change goes into an investment account. This feature, which has drawn a passionately devoted customer base (with over nine million sign ups as of this writing)[30]...is available at virtually every bank.

So what's the secret? Acorns isn't selling round up as a feature. They aren't leading with the product. They have created shared value. They are offering customers a chance to "Grow your oak!" What Acorns is actually selling is the ability to grow stronger and more financially secure.

---

[30] https://www.acorns.com/

Fintechs have found value agreement, which has allowed them to leapfrog some of the big banks. It doesn't matter if you view your bank, product, or service as highly valuable if that view is not shared by your audience.

REAL WORLD EXAMPLE: HARLEY DAVIDSON

What is Harley Davidson's product? Motorcycles. But do they only talk about motorcycles in their ads? Do their commercials focus on engine specs? Not so much.

Motorcycles are the product, but they aren't the brand—because product is not brand.

So what is Harley Davidson's brand?

Freedom.

Their mission statement reads: "More than building machines, we stand for the timeless pursuit of adventure. Freedom for the soul."

Remember, a product is just a delivery mechanism. It's how you deliver your brand and experience, but it isn't how you define it. You can't define your bank through product.

There are plenty of people in the industry who have modernized their marketing strategies and now say, "It's not about rates." And they're right. But this may be oversimplifying the issue. A more nuanced approach would be to acknowledge that rates and products absolutely do matter in the context of what they enable a customer to do.

In the world of Harley Davidson, that focus on outcome (through product) looks like this: "Today, we continue to define motorcycle culture and lifestyle, evoking soul-stirring emotion reflected in every product and experience we deliver—like we have for well over a century and will for generations to come."

This is an example of brand-first thinking, focusing on the experience that the product creates as well as the context that experience happens in. In order to do this, you have to truly leverage your data, place product in the proper place, and commit to creating a shared unit of value (in Harley's case, that value is freedom).

KEY TAKEAWAYS

Remember, Product Isn't What It Used to Be

1. **Loyalty is not what it used to be either:** points and prizes are transactional, making emotional connections is what matters.

2. **Product is not brand:** products deliver your brand, but don't define it.

3. **Product is not a language:** Customers don't speak banking. Change the conversation to focus on what products do, not what they are.

4. **Outcomes trump features, functions, and toasters:** product is the vehicle to deliver value, not the value itself.

5. **A mission statement is not a mission:** There's a limit to mission statements. But there's no limit to a mission.

6. **Imagine if your mission was your product:** building a brand around an authentic mission is profitable, meaning-ful, and valuable.

7. **The future of value is shared value:** it doesn't matter if you view your bank, product, or service as highly valuable if that view is not shared by your audience.

PRINCIPLE 04

Remember, **Product Isn't What It Used to Be**

REMEMBER

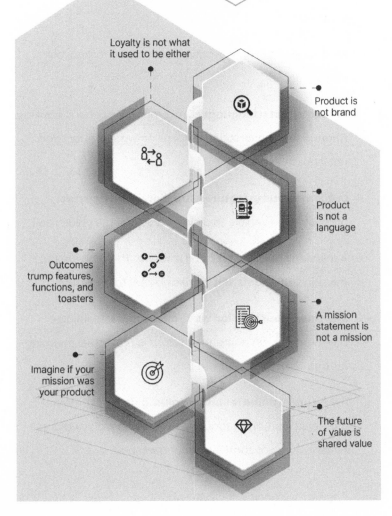

Loyalty is not what
it used to be either

Product is
not brand

Product
is not a
language

Outcomes
trump features,
functions, and
toasters

A mission
statement is
not a mission

Imagine if your
mission was
your product

The future
of value is
shared value

THINK LIKE A BRAND, NOT A BANK

Chapter 6

PRINCIPLE FIVE: COACH AND COMPOSE

"This is how you do it: you sit down at the keyboard and you put one word after another until it's done. It's that easy, and that hard."

—Neil Gaiman

YOU'VE PUT IN THE WORK, and it's time to have some fun.

This chapter explores how a brand-first mindset creates the energy to compose new services, experiences, and outcomes, and how to coach your organization and customers to embrace them. Coaching and composing are critical to bringing new business models to market and attracting new market segments.

"I skipped the earlier principles; is that cool?"

No. That is not cool. You are missing out.

We recognize that you want to get to the fun stuff—creating new experiences—but there's a reason we presented our principles in a specific order.

Innovation needs a place to take root. Creating a brand-first mindset, remixing, and embracing the tension of becoming outcome focused helps make this happen. The mindset shifts brought about by the previous principles are what give your organization the permission and ability to transform.

To help jumpstart your creativity, it might help to look at examples of others who are composing new experiences. What does this creativity look like in the real world?

REAL WORLD EXAMPLE: A MOONSHOT IN UTAH

In the 1960s, when NASA was tackling the question of how to put a man on the moon, they set up a unit—the Apollo team—to work exclusively on that challenge. The idea was that if a team is isolated from all the other headaches of an organization, they can better focus on their mission. And it worked. By 1969, NASA had their brave astronauts playing golf on the moon. Mission accomplished!

Ever since the success of Apollo 11, it has become customary to label breakthroughs a *moonshot*. The mission to invent a driverless car is a moonshot. The race to develop a gene therapy to fight cancer is a moonshot. And in each of these examples, there is a smaller, dedicated team assigned to nothing but their singular mission.

So why not try this in the financial sector? Why not apply the concept of a moonshot team to developing breakthroughs in the banking industry?

It's already happening.

The executive director of digital banking at one of Utah's largest banks was given the green light to set up his own moonshot team. He put together a maverick unit of coworkers to build a new brand within a separate division. The team's moonshot mission was to create extraordinary digital first experiences for aspiring small business owners. Innovation number one was creating a digital bank that offers live support from real people, and the option to choose your personal banking team. Next, they focused on creating a fully integrated job quotation system that was automatically linked to the bank and a simplified cash flow projection tool.

And that's just the beginning of their innovation journey. Because the team is walled off from their parent company, they have the freedom to compose new experiences without being judged against the norms or traditions of an $85 billion bank that was founded over a century ago. To put that in *Think Like a Brand* language...they don't have to change a 150 year old mindset for 10,000 employees. Instead, a moonshot team can focus on the brand-first mindset with a core team of less than a dozen people.

This moonshot team operates like an independent think tank, composing innovative new experiences that challenge the status quo. And the beauty of this moonshot setup is that, if the team creates something brilliant and viable, it can be used by the entire organization.

We also have our eye on Maast, a "very flexible, configurable, brandable, embedded finance platform" from Synovus.[31] Because Synovus is a 250 branch behemoth with over 130 years of history in the South, Maast is a moonshot opportunity to compose new experiences under a new brand without rocking the boat of their established institution.

COUNTRY MUSIC, WHISKEY, AND...SOCCER?

When someone says Tennessee, several images come to mind. Jack Daniels whiskey, Dolly Parton and country music, Beale Street in Memphis, and hot chicken in Nashville. But...soccer?

---

[31] https://www.fool.com/earnings/call-transcripts/2022/01/20/synovus-financial-snv-q4-2021-earnings-call-transc/

Uh, no.

So, it may have come as a shock to casual observers when Nashville, Tennessee, was awarded a Major League Soccer franchise in 2017. Nashville somehow convinced the league to expand to a state more known for steel guitars than soccer, and they beat out eleven other cities to do it—including some cities that had been working toward an MLS franchise for a decade.

Two years before being awarded the MLS franchise, Nashville didn't even have a semipro team. In fact, they barely had an amateur team—Nashville FC, a one-year-old club cruising to a lackluster fourth place in their conference.

So how did they pull it off? How did they persuade MLS to give them a top level soccer franchise?

They composed an experience.

Marcus Whitney, a longtime Nashville entrepreneur and venture capitalist, was the chairman of the city's amateur team. With a history of co-founding Nashville-area startups, Whitney had an eye for spotting opportunities. Yes, Tennessee was known for other things. Yes, football was still much more popular than soccer there. But Whitney saw Nashville changing. He saw younger generations pouring in. He saw the city's international community growing.

Whitney partnered with two other business executives to launch a new team, Nashville SC. They bought out the amateur team's name, logo, and color scheme, and landed a spot in the United Soccer League (USL), a pro league two levels below MLS.[32] But they didn't stop there. They knew that teams often languished in the lower divisions of American soccer for years, so they immediately brought in some big guns to signal that they had higher aspirations. First, they got John Ingram, a well-known Nashville billionaire, to become a majority owner in the team.[33] Next, they signed a former MLS coach (Gary Smith) to manage the club.[34]

With an owner worth $4.2 billion and a coach who had already won an MLS Cup, Nashville SC was sending a message to the MLS—this is not a hobby for us.

In 2017, when Nashville put forward a bid for an MLS franchise, they were competing with eleven other cities, including five that already had soccer clubs playing in a higher division than they were.[35]

---

[32] https://www.tennessean.com/story/news/local/2016/05/19/nashville-awarded-united-soccer-league-franchise/84559766/

[33] https://www.tennessean.com/story/news/2016/12/20/businessman-john-ingram-lead-nashvilles-major-league-soccer-bid/95654904/

[34] https://www.tennessean.com/story/sports/2017/04/12/gary-smith-nashville-soccer/100368758/

[35] https://www.si.com/soccer/2016/12/21/mls-expansion-prospective-cities-bids-28-teams

But Whitney and the Nashville soccer supporters knew they had something great. And they composed an experience for their prospective customer—the MLS—to see what they saw in their city. They wanted the league to see the advantages of their location: the changing demographics, the infrastructure (three interstates and an international airport), the rapid growth of the area. But most of all...

They took the MLS executives around the city to let them experience the intangibles of Nashville. The energy. The excitement. The momentum of a city on the rise. They created an experience that led the MLS to believe that if they didn't give Nashville a franchise, they'd be missing out.

Whitney and the Nashville SC organization built a solid product, backed by a solid investment, but also made the vitality of the city itself part of the composition.

But what exactly does coaching mean in the context of banking experiences?

COMPOSING FOR A NARROW SEGMENT

Banking with a generic appeal will inevitably become a commodity instead of a value-added service. And these institutions can't be completely customer centric because their ideal customer is everyone. How can you design a perfect experience that's perfect for everyone?

You can't.

We recently worked with a bank that was interested in reaching an untapped market. They showed us data indicating that, in the areas where they had branches, 36 percent of the population was Hispanic.

"Hispanic" seemed like a fairly broad category, so we asked them, "Specifically who in the 'Hispanic' community are you targeting?"

"The whole 36 percent!" they said.

We did the math. "That's literally millions of people."

"I know, right?" They were excited.

When a financial institution sees a large, untapped market, the tendency is to go after the entire group. But here's the thing: They aren't a group. They are millions of individuals.

And some of those individuals aren't wild about the term "Hispanic." (And some are gay, and some are wealthy, and some are disabled, and some are Republicans, and some are half Asian, and some love bowling...) There is no single experience that could possibly appeal to all of these individuals.

Attempting to reach out to a broad swath of a population with a generic appeal, even if it is "targeted," is bank thinking instead of brand thinking.

Here is an example of approaching a large addressable market with a brand lens....

In October of 2021, Mastercard introduced a new type of card for the visually impaired: the Touch Card. These new cards allow customers to quickly distinguish their credit card from their debit card or prepaid card. Unique notches on each different type of card (square, rounded, or triangular) offer a tactile way to tell them apart.[36]

We can't assume that we can solve problems for people of a community if we haven't had the conversations to create emotional connection and collaboration on the challenges that need to be solved. Many organizations try to appeal to subsets of the population by being more accessible to that demographic.

But you can't assume accessibility (which is a product-first approach) means attractive.

---

[36] https://www.mastercard.com/news/press/2021/october/mastercard-introduces-accessible-card-for-blind-and-partially-sighted-people/

COACH TO CHANGE

We all know that a brainstorming session isn't over when the meeting adjourns. That's just the beginning of the process. Those ideas for amazing new customer experiences still have a long way to go to become a reality. And they won't ever make it to the light of day without someone in your organization coaching the team, and shepherding the changes toward implementation.

While compose is the part of the process that creates cool new ideas for the organization, coach is the next step, which draws a roadmap between vision and reality.

The truth is, most banks have no shortage of ideas. So why don't these ideas see the light of day? Were they not good enough? Were they too hard to implement?

Not at all. There was nothing wrong with the ideas. The compose part was just fine. What was missing was someone coaching the team to make the idea a reality. (And we're dying to use a sports analogy here, but we promised ourselves we wouldn't do that.)

If you've put in the time and effort to compose great ideas, you need someone to coach them into reality. Someone to take them off the page, away from a to-do list, and into motion. Someone has to get the rest of the organization on board, set a launch date, and explain it to the customer.

Do changes ever take place without great coaching? Sure. But, let's take the Nashville SC example. Nashville won the bid, but it wasn't just the site visit that landed them the franchise. They had to coach their customer (MLS) to take advantage of that Nashville experience. They coached the MLS to see there was a shared unit of value for the city and the league.

And, they continue to coach Nashville SC fans, Nashville residents, and the broader MLS community on the value of the franchise; great coaching, like great brands, never ends.

COACHING MINDSET

Take a look at weight loss statistics. Yep. Weight loss statistics. According to a 2003 study, people who tried self-help programs were not nearly as successful as people who were attending weekly meetings of a commercial weight loss program (such as Weight Watchers). In fact, people who were getting the weekly coaching and the accountability of regular check-ins lost three times as much weight as those who tried to go it alone.[37]

It's just human nature. People are more likely to change when they have a coach.

---

[37] https://pubmed.ncbi.nlm.nih.gov/12684357/

And the same is true of organizations. Just like individuals, they must overcome bad habits, stay dedicated, and focus on the outcomes. Nothing keeps a person—or company—focused like great coaching.

But what if a lack of coaching is endemic to your organization?

You can change that.

A coaching culture can be nurtured within an institution because coaching tactics are learned behaviors. Instead of sitting back and saying, "We just don't do anything with our great ideas," it's time to change your organization's mindset.

Several years back, Microsoft launched an initiative to foster a customer-centric attitude in its employees. They called it the customer champions program.[38] They took key team members out of their regular roles and gave them intense training to better understand Microsoft as seen through the eyes of the customer. The trainees had access to customer research, listened to customer calls, and were schooled on the needs and motivations of Microsoft customers.

After the program, the trainees went back to their regular day jobs as customer champions and coached their coworkers to talk about customers in every meeting. They provided customer data to

---

[38] https://www.stickyminds.com/presentation/rise-customer-champions

their teams to explore and support every decision around product, service, or marketing campaign. The program was accredited with driving significant increases in customer advocacy, satisfaction, and profitability across the business.

The coaching mindset can also come from outside the organization.

We've heard countless financial institutions tell us that they are resource constrained. If you don't have the budget or personnel to create coaching internally, tap into an external coaching community. There are a multitude of great coaches out there like James Robert Lay, Founder of the Digital Growth Institute, who have written playbooks on how to coach a team to move innovations toward the finish line. Many of these coaches offer passionate, knowledgeable, and experienced advice—and it's often available for free.

HOW TO COACH CUSTOMERS

Marstone is a wealth management platform that has welcomed the role of being a digital coach to their customers. They're taking the old method of financial advice (in person, heavy paperwork, and pressured decision making) and reshaping it so that the customer has more control and can set the pace.

Marstone is coaching their customers to map out their life goals and providing the data and information that are pertinent to those goals. They're coaching customers to think for themselves. They're coaching customers to ask the right questions. And they're coaching their customers to take a leadership role in their own financial decisions.

When we take a traditional experience in the financial world and replace it with something entirely new, there will inevitably be a learning curve.

Don't shy away from new experiences for your customers because you think they won't get it, or because you think they might need a small nudge to adopt it.

Let's not forget—most people were content going to Blockbuster stores to rent movies until Netflix coached them into adopting a different experience.

Nashville residents were content with football and hockey until the Nashville SC organization coached them to embrace a new sports experience. (Over 59,000 people attended their opening game.)[39]

At Apple Stores, the Genius Bar still coaches all day, every day.

---

[39] https://www.nashvillesc.com/news/nashville-sc-breaks-tennessee-soccer-attendance-record-59069-hand-mls-debut

WHEN IT CLICKS

Composing is all about creating new experiences for your customer by reimagining what even the most basic elements of your institution can be. You get to look at old experiences from new angles, and question why some traditional experiences haven't evolved.

We recently met with a credit union in the Southeast that wanted to serve all of the people of their state. They were acutely aware that the typical member (white, middle class) did not reflect the population of their region, so they wanted to reach out to people in rural areas, people with lower incomes, and those with low literacy rates. They had wanted to reach these underserved populations for years.

Without a coach and compose method in place, they had experimented with bilingual tellers and new branches, but nothing had taken hold.

So, we started the process with a Mindset Matters workshop—using every principle in this book—to get them out of bank thinking and into brand thinking.

Here's what we heard:

- Instead of new branches, one team member suggested putting branch experiences in spaces that already have

the trust of underserved populations in rural areas—
places like public libraries and churches.

- Instead of bilingual tellers in a traditional branch, these
  tellers could work out of the public library for four hours
  a week because that's where people were going to use
  the internet.

- Instead of holding events at an existing branch, they could
  offer banking services at farmers markets—not just to sign
  people up, but to help them with actual banking.

They were composing their hearts out.

We pointed out that the ideas they had just generated were actually
easier to implement than some of the initiatives they had already
attempted. So we asked them, "Why haven't you done any of these
new ideas?"

They responded: "We've never gotten excited about it before."

So okay. They were excited now. It was time to make sure that
coaching was in place so that the ideas wouldn't die after the meeting adjourned.

We had the team pick one of their favorite ideas, then we put them
on the spot. "So how will this move forward? Who's going to run

this process? Who's going to be the person that wakes up every day thinking about this?"

Next, we discussed the practical obstacles that they would probably face. And it was interesting… obstacles that had felt insurmountable before (when they thought their ideas were just pipe dreams), now seemed less daunting. The ideas seemed more possible because we coached them through it.

When these ideas become reality, will the members need some coaching? Sure. Will they be confused to see a bank in a blood-mobile? Undoubtedly! But with a little coaching, they'll come around. And once customers realize how the credit union will improve their lives, the word will spread in the community.

KEY TAKEAWAYS

Coach and Compose

1. **Don't be afraid to take a moonshot:** Give yourself space to compose new experiences without rocking the boat. Protect your creativity from the realities of running the bank.

2. **You don't have to be Beethoven to compose the future you want:** Composing is about putting together existing resources to tell a different story. Look around you with fresh eyes, and you will be surprised what you can create.

3. **Some of the best compositions only have four chords, just ask the Beatles:** Don't try to be everything to everyone. Find a niche and play it flawlessly.

4. **Weightwatchers and Microsoft know what they're doing:** successful brands know the importance of supporting people to adapt to change.

5. **Everybody needs a little coaching now and again:** Growth and innovation means doing things differently. You'll need to coach yourself, your teams, and your customers to make sure everyone gets value from the experiences you compose.

 PRINCIPLE 05

Coach and Compose

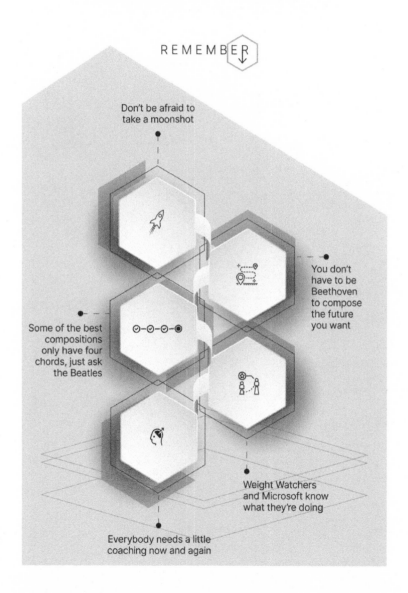

REMEMBER

Don't be afraid to take a moonshot

You don't have to be Beethoven to compose the future you want

Some of the best compositions only have four chords, just ask the Beatles

Weight Watchers and Microsoft know what they're doing

Everybody needs a little coaching now and again

CONCLUSION

WE BELIEVE THE FINANCIAL INDUSTRY CAN shift its mind-set, build trust, innovate, and grow by following the principles we laid out in this book. In fact, by looking at the market from a new perspective and putting in the work, banks and credit unions can build the loyalty and affinity evoked by the world's favorite brands.

Before an organization can tackle the principles of becoming a brand, however, they must master the brand-first mindset. This means they have to let go of bank-first thinking, and figure out how to connect with people on an emotional level. It means that the organization has to break through its limiting beliefs, and it means that the entire company—not just the marketing department—will have to internalize what the organization stands for. It isn't easy to change the mindset of an entire organization, but it can be done. You own your company's mindset, so you don't need a consultant or expensive new technology to make a change.

Once your organization starts to get the hang of the brand-first mindset, and begins to brainstorm ways to change, there will be tension. In fact, outright contradictions will emerge. Embrace that tension. Lean into the fear of change, and tackle those contradictions with confidence. You may discover epic breakthroughs on the other side.

When you do generate a brilliant new idea that could strengthen your brand, you might have to do the counterintuitive thing to launch it. To enhance your bank's digital experience, for example, you might have to speak to customers face-to-face. To connect with your customers better, you may have to discard binary thinking and operate in the gray area between two categories.

Remember—you don't have to start from scratch. Big changes can come from remixing the raw materials you already have in your organization. Most banks and credit unions already have the personnel and technology to make new ideas work, so use what's at your disposal in creative ways. Whether you're creating a new type of account for a gig worker or taking a consumer product and applying it to corporations, you don't have to reinvent the wheel. Sometimes, the best new ideas are just old ideas with a twist. Harnessing the power of the remix to launch a new idea can also take away much of the anxiety that comes with change, because using an organization's existing assets makes the decisions feel smaller.

You can never stop getting to know your customer. Don't assume that you know them well just because you know their demographics, or because they're a longtime customer. If you're not sure if a new concept will create an emotional connection with people, just try it. But don't dwell on ideas that don't work. Just test, learn, and move on. And if you are truly a brand rebel, consider changing the very structure of your organization. Give some thought to elevating customer experience leaders in your corporate hierarchy and placing customer experience at the heart of every decision you make.

Financial institutions use their oceans of data to keep track of customer demographics, but a brand uses data to identify trends and predictors. Brands use data to understand not only what customers want now, but what they might want five years from now. New upstart fintechs are using data to connect with consumers instead of pigeonhole them, and banks should take note. Traditional financial institutions should view fintechs as industry catalysts instead of competitors. There's a lot to learn from the upstarts in our industry, including the new and evolving needs of modern customers.

In the past, banks were defined by their products—their accounts, loans, and rates. But to become a beloved brand, a financial institution has to go beyond the product and think in terms of a customer's experience. Products are still important, of course, but they are just one side of the equation. A brand thinks of the other side as well: what the customer values. True brand success comes when a bank identifies a shared unit of value with the customer and collaborates with them to define an outcome that is beneficial to both customer and the bank.

When an organization has a brand mindset, leans into contradictions, and seeks shared outcomes with their customers, the fun really begins. A brand composes exciting new experiences and services for customers based on shared values. When you create outcomes that align with the values of the customer and the brand, you can coach your team to make the idea a reality, then coach the customer to adopt the new experience. Coaching and composing new experiences can attract new market segments or launch entirely new business models.

Brands go beyond caring about their customers. They obsess. If you aim to be a brand instead of just a bank, you can't see your customers as merely bank customers. You have to see them as whole people, with passions, dreams, disappointments, and desires. A true brand learns the obsessions of their customers and shares a mission with them based on those obsessions.

When you obsess about your customer and find a shared mission with your customers, they will start to obsess over you. Your customers will become more than customers. They will evangelize on your behalf.

We've covered a lot of ground together, from why marketers need a seat at the strategy table, to the monetary value added by a brand. And nowhere in this book has the shift from bank to brand been described as easy. But it is necessary. If we want to stay relevant in a changing industry, we have to embrace a mission based, outcome-focused approach that sparks an emotional connection with customers—and we believe YOU can do it!

If you only remember three things from this book, hold on to these:

- Mindset matters. You have to establish a brand-first mindset internally before you can connect as a brand.

- You need brand values to create brand value. Define what your brand stands for and don't compromise. Customers will connect with your mission.

- Things are not changing, they've already changed.

As you continue your journey toward thinking like a brand, not a bank, let us know how it's going! We'd love to hear your updates, questions, or anecdotes. Give this book to a colleague or friend who you think could also benefit. We'll post our updates as well at www.thinklikeabrandbook.com.

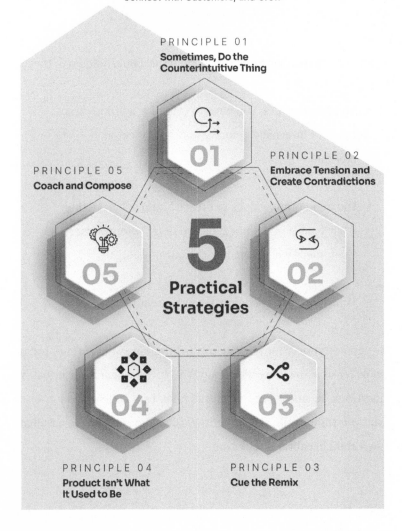

ACKNOWLEDGMENTS

WE WOULD LIKE TO THANK EVERYONE who allowed us to interview them for this book:

- Jody Guetter

- John Janclaes

- Justin Dunn

- Rilla Delorier

- Corey LeBlanc

- Maurice Moody

- Walter "Chip" Hasselbring III

- Linda Hamilton

- Christine Alemany

- Derik Sutton

- Margaret Hartigan

The amazing team at Scribe Media: Aleks, Erin, Oceana, and Meghan. Aleks, thank you for encouraging and believing in us (often more so than we believed in ourselves).

For James Robert Lay, who introduced us to Scribe Media and gave so much of his time, insight, and wisdom.

For Catherine DeStasio who helped us frame the initial draft and supported us along the way.

For Sarah Schaper for her keen design eye and contributions.

For Jeremy Bagley for giving us our first feedback.

For Billee Howard for her encouragement and no nonsense advice.

For our friend Sangita at GiftSuite for the book swag.

The wonderful hospitality of Jeannie and Bubba at The Reserve at Greenleaf.

All those who signed up early to show support for this book—thank you!

For those who continue to support the book (and us) on social media.

FROM ALLISON

I would especially like to thank (again) my friend and mentor Jeffery Kendall for believing in me; I hope the book makes you proud.

This book, and really everything else, would not be possible without the support of my family and friends. Sara, thanks for all the big dawg support. Michael and Ozlem, thank you for always reading with love. Bill, thank you for the prayers and encouragement. Grandma, thank you for saying, "I always knew you would do something good." Mom, thanks for moving mountains for me my entire life and being the original Quill and Scroll. Aunt Lucy and Uncle Bill, thanks for being so excited for me; it means a lot. To the Parker and Gercans families: I am grateful for your love and support. Choco, I know you are a dog and can't read, but thanks for always being at my feet during this process.

Kerri, thanks for being my flight companion—I hope to read your book soon! Alana, thank you for literally being the infrastructure behind the book. Cassie, I truly could not have done this without your belief. To my Red Velvet Events friends, thank you for being (more) excited about this than I was at times. Thanks to my favorite Texans, Dave and Tanner Mayo. True gratitude for the years of encouragement from my friends Sam Kilmer and Ron Shevlin. Fan girl gratitude to Rilla Delorier—I admire you more than you know! Deep appreciation to Dr. Pierce for helping me work through life. Thank you to Marcus Whitney for inspiring me before we even met, and for your support of other authors.

To my coauthor (sounds so cool!) Liz High, I can't thank you enough for going on this journey with me. You inspire me, and I feel like we have really accomplished something together that will help others. Thank you for the days, nights, and weekends you put into the project—it's a process and a friendship that I will never forget.

Finally, to the three that bring me joy, acceptance, and laughter …Vicki, Jackson, and Henry. Vicki, it goes without saying that our family would literally be nothing without you. Thank you for being my biggest supporter, and for the hours hanging out with the kids so I could write. I love you.

Henry and Jackson, I don't know when or if you will read this book, but we talked about it a lot at meals and you gave me good advice. You are my sweet potatoes and I love you.

FROM LIZ

I would like to thank all of the people in my life that I have been ignoring as I focused on the book. There are too many to mention, but I will see you all in a bar of your choice soon.

This would not have happened without the mentorship and friendship of my coauthor (yes, it does sound cool!), Allison Netzer. Your uncompromising commitment to pushing me to do better and to pursue my goals is incredibly empowering. There are not enough words to express my gratitude for the time, resources, and creative conversations we have had while writing the book. Thank you.

Most importantly, I am grateful to my family—Sam, Sapphire, and Scarlet—who have put up with missed lunches, late dinners, and my absence from family life while my head was stuck in the manuscript. Thank you for being supportive every day, and for your advice on everything from the cover, my headshot, to the title, and swag options. Sorry there are no, "Think Like a Brand" socks—maybe for the next book! I love and appreciate you all.

Brand is powerful.

Forget bank-first thinking.

Brand is not soft and fluffy.

Get in touch with your feelings.

Think of Samsung with a side of Apple.

Brand is not a marketing exercise.

Your windshield is bigger than your rearview for a reason.

Everything builds.

Be open to odd.

Search for spaces.

Don't be customer first.

Quit fighting fintechs.

Remake meaningful moments.

Beautiful brands are born
from tension.

Modernize your roles.

Keep it simple.

Stop when you get to yes.

Make your decisions smaller.

Good things can happen in silos;
great things happen when
you break them down.

Don't ask what can we do,
ask what could we do.

Make your financial products
into brand experience.

If it doesn't work, ditch it.

Loyalty is not what it used
to be either.

Product is not brand.

Product is not a language.

Outcomes trump features, functions,
and toasters.

A mission statement is not a mission.

Imagine if your mission was
your product.

The future of value is shared value.

Thinking like a brand
STARTS NOW.

Made in the USA
Las Vegas, NV
04 April 2023

70151039R00111